P9-BJB-222

WORLD PASS

Expanding English Fluency

Susan Stempleski
James R. Morgan
Nancy Douglas
Kristin L. Johannsen

HEINLE
CENGAGE Learning

Australia • Brazil • Japan • Korea • Mexico • Singapore • Spain • United Kingdom • United States

HEINLE
CENGAGE Learning

World Pass Upper-Intermediate,
Student Book
Susan Stempleski
James R. Morgan, Nancy Douglas,
Kristin L. Johannsen

Publisher: Christopher Wenger
Director of Content Development:
Anita Raducanu
Director of Product Marketing: Amy Mabley
Acquisitions Editor: Mary Sutton-Paul
Developmental Editor: Rebecca Klevberg
Associate Editor: Christine Galvin-Combet
Editotial Assistant: Bridget McLaughlin
Content Project Manager: Tan Jin Hock
Sr. Print Buyer: Mary Beth Hennebury
International Marketing Manager: Ian Martin
Contributing Development Editor:
Ellen Kisslinger
Compositor: CHROME Media Pte. Ltd.
Photo Researcher: Christopher Hanzie
Illustrator: Raketshop Design Studio
(Philippines)
Cover/Text Designer: CHROME Media Pte. Ltd.
Cover Images: Corbis
Text Credits
Page 7: "Rules of the Game," from THE JOY LUCK CLUB by Amy Tan,
copyright ©1989 by Amy Tan. Used by permission of G.P. Putnam's
Sons, a division of Penguin Group (USA) Inc.; page 9: Adapted from
"The Monkey's Paw" (1902) from The Lady of the Barge 6th ed.
Published in 1906 by W.W. Jacobs, Harper & Brothers, Publishers,
London and New York; page 84: Adapted from "Gorilla-Suited
Prankster Caught," Ananova.com, October 13, 2004. Used by
permission of Ananova, Ltd.

Photo Credits
Unless otherwise stated, all photos are from PhotoDisc, Inc. Digital
Imagery © copyright 2005 PhotoDisc, Inc. and TYA Inc. Photos
from other sources: page 4: (top) Royalty-Free/CORBIS, (bottom)
Richard T. Nowitz/CORBIS; page 5: Janet Jarman/CORBIS; page 6:
Gabe Palmer/CORBIS; page 21: METRO AG; page 29: Royalty-Free/
CORBIS; page 30: (bottom) Royalty-Free/CORBIS; page 43: Arko
Datta/Reuters/Landov; page 53: Royalty-Free/CORBIS; page 54: (left)
Jim Thompson House & Museum, (right) Chris Lisle/CORBIS; page 55:
Jim Thompson House & Museum; page 56: Randy Faris/CORBIS; page
83: (right) Royalty-Free/Doug Menuez/Photodisc; page 87: Royalty-
Free/CORBIS; page 102: (bottom) Sean Bermingham; page 105:
Lucy Nicholson/Reuters/Landov; page 131: Patrik Giardino/CORBIS;
page 132: Royalty-Free/CORBIS; page 140: (bottom) Joseph Sohm,
ChromoSohm Inc./CORBIS; page 142: Jim Sugar/CORBIS; page 143:
Royalty-Free/Don Farrall/Photodisc; page 144: Royalty-Free/CORBIS;
page 147: (left) Punit Paranjpe/Reuters/Landov, (right) Boris Roessler/
EPA/Landov

The CNN® logo is a registered trademark of CNN:
© & ® 2005. Cable News Network LP, LLLP. A Time
Warner Company. All Rights Reserved.

Every effort has been made to trace all sources of
illustrations/photos/information in this book, but
if any have been inadvertently overlooked, the
publisher will be pleased to make the necessary
arrangements at the first opportunity.

ISBN-13: 978-0-8384-0669-4

ISBN-10: 0-8384-0669-6

Heinle
20 Channel Center Street,
Boston, MA 02210
USA

Cengage Learning is a leading provider of customized learning solutions with
office locations around the globe, including Singapore, the United Kingdom,
Australia, Mexico, Brazil and Japan. Locate our local office at:
international.cengage.com/region

Cengage Learning products are represented in Canada by Nelson Education, Ltd.

Visit Heinle online at **elt.heinle.com**
Visit our corporate website at **cengage.com**

Printed in China
9 10 12 11 10

Acknowledgments

We would firstly like to thank the educators who provided invaluable feedback throughout the development of the *World Pass* series:

Byung-kyoo Ahn, Chonnam National University; Elisabeth Blom, Casa Thomas Jefferson; Grazyna Anna Bonomi; Vera Burlamaqui Bradford, Instituto Brasil-Estados Unidos; Araceli Cabanillas Carrasco, Universidad Autónoma de Sinaloa; Silvania Capua Carvalho, State University of Feira de Santana; Tânia Branco Cavaignac, Casa Branca Idiomas; Kyung-whan Cha, Chung-Ang University; Chwun-li Chen, Shih Chien University; María Teresa Fátima Encinas, Universidad Iberoamericana-Puebla and Universidad Autónoma de Puebla; Sandra Gaviria, Universidad EAFIT; Marina González, Instituto de Lenguas Modernas; Frank Graziani, Tokai University; Chi-ying Fione Huang, Ming Chuan University; Shu-fen Huang (Jessie), Chung Hua University; Tsai, Shwu Hui (Ellen), Chung Kuo Institute of Technology and Commerce; Connie R. Johnson, Universidad de las Américas-Puebla; Diana Jones, Instituto Angloamericano; Annette Kaye, Kyoritsu Women's University; Lee, Kil-ryoung, Yeungnam University; David Kluge, Kinjo Gakuin University; Nancy H. Lake; Hyunoo Lee, Inha University; Amy Peijung Lee, Hsuan Chuang College; Hsiu-Yun Liao, Chinese Culture University; Yuh-Huey Gladys Lin, Chung Hua University; Eleanor Occeña, Universitaria de Idiomas, Universidad Autónoma del Estado de Hidalgo; Laura Pérez Palacio, Tecnológico de Monterrey; Doraci Perez Mak, União Cultural Brasil-Estados Unidos; Mae-Ran Park, Pukyong National University; Joo-Kyung Park, Honam University; Bill Pellowe, Kinki University; Margareth Perucci, Sociedade Brasileira de Cultura Inglesa; Nevitt Reagan, Kansai Gaidai University; Lesley D. Riley, Kanazawa Institute of Technology; Ramiro Luna Rivera, Tecnológico de Monterrey, Prepa; Marie Adele Ryan, Associação Alumni; Michael Shawback, Ritsumeikan University; Kathryn Singh, ITESM; Grant Trew, Nova Group; Michael Wu, Chung Hua University, Carmen Pulido Alcaraz, Instituto Cultural Mexico-Norteamericano, Guadalajara; Maria Isabel de Souza Lima Baracat, Centro de Comunicação Inglesa, Garça; João Alfredo Bergmann, Instituto Cultural Brasileiro Norte-Americano, Porto Alegre; Elisabeth Blom, Casa Thomas Jefferson, Brasília; Flávia Carneiro - Associação Brasil América; Salvador Enriquez Casteñeda, Instituto Cultural Mexico-Norteamericano, Guadalajara; Ronaldo Couto, SBS, São Paulo; Maria Amélia Carvalho Fonseca, Centro Cultural Brasil-Estados Unidos, Belém; Henry W. Grant, Centro Cultural Brasil-Estados Unidos, Campinas; Leticia Adelina Ruiz Guerrero, ITESO, Guadalajara; Brian Lawrence Kilkenny, PrepaTec, Guadalajara; Lunalva de Fátima Lacerda, Cooplem, Brasília; Raquel Lambert, CCBEU - Centro Cultural Brasil Estados Unidos de Franca; Alberto Hernandez Medina, M. Ed., Tecnológico de Monterrey, Guadalajara; Michelle Merritt-Ascencio, University of Guadalajara; Evania A. Netto, ICBEU - São José dos Campos; Janette Carvalhinho de Oliveira, Universidade Federal do Espírito Santo, Vitória; Ane Cibele Palma, CCBEU/Interamericano, Curitiba; Danielle Rêgo, ICBEU - MA; Marie Adele Ryan, Associação Alumni, São Paulo; Hector Sanchez, PROULEX, Guadalajara; Dixie Santana, Universidad Panamericana, Guadalajara; Rodrigo Santana, CCBEU/Goiânia; Debora Schisler, SEVEN English & Español, São Paulo; Sávio Siqueira, ACBEU Salvador; Eric Tejeda, PROULEX, Guadalajara; Carlos Eduardo Tristão, DISAL; Joaquin Romero Vázquez, Tec de Monterrey, Guadalajara; Liliana Villalobos ME, Universidad Marista de Guadalajara, Universidad de Guadalajara

---

A great many people participated in the making of the *World Pass* series. In particular I would like to thank the authors, Nancy Douglas and James Morgan, for all their hard work, creativity, and good humor. I also extend special thanks to development editor Ellen Kisslinger. Thanks are also due to publisher Chris Wenger, acquisitions editor Mary Sutton-Paul, and all the other wonderful people at Heinle who have worked so hard on this project. I am also very grateful to the many reviewers around the world, whose insightful comments on early drafts of the *World Pass* materials were much appreciated.

Susan Stempleski

We'd like to extend a very special thank you to Chris Wenger at Heinle for spearheading the project and providing leadership, support, and guidance throughout the development of the series. Jean Pender and Ellen Kisslinger edited our materials with speed, precision, and a sense of humor. Susan Stempleski's extensive experience was reflected in her invaluable feedback that helped to shape the material in this book.

Thanks also go to those on the editorial, production, and support teams who helped to make this book happen: Anita Raducanu, Sally Giangrande, Jin-Hock Tan, Bridget McLaughlin, Christine Galvin-Combet, Rebecca Klevberg, Mary Sutton-Paul, and their colleagues in Asia and Latin America.

I would also like to thank my parents Alexander and Patricia, for their love and encouragement and to my husband Jorge and daughter Jasmine—thank you for your patience and faith in me. I couldn't have done this without you!
Nancy Douglas

I would also like to thank my mother, France P. Morgan, for her unflagging support and my father, Lee Morgan Jr., for instilling the love of language and learning in me.
James R. Morgan

I would like to thank my husband, Kevin Millham, for his support and saintly patience.
Kristin L. Johannsen

To the Student

Welcome to *World Pass*! The main goal of this two-level, upper-intermediate/advanced level series is to help you increase your fluency in English. By fluency, I mean the ability to say what you want in more than one way, and to communicate your ideas clearly, confidently, and easily. To help students increase their fluency, *World Pass* focuses on dynamic vocabulary building, essential grammar, and stimulating listening, speaking, and writing activities that emphasize the language people need for real world communication. Features of *World Pass* that emphasize the development of oral and written fluency include the following:

- Vocabulary Focus sections. A *Vocabulary Focus* section opens each of the 12 main units and presents topic-related vocabulary along with opportunities to practice using the new words and expressions in a variety of ways. The section includes a "Vocabulary Builder" activity that helps you expand your vocabulary through the use of a particular vocabulary-building tool (e.g., word families, root words, or compound nouns). Many of the *Vocabulary Focus* sections conclude with an "Ask & Answer" task that can be used as a basis for discussion by pairs, groups, or whole classes of students, and provides opportunities to actively use new vocabulary to express personal ideas, opinions, and experiences.

- Listening sections. To become a fluent speaker, you need to be a fluent listener. These sections provide opportunities for you to improve your listening comprehension through active practice with a variety of materials, such as interviews, news reports, and discussions. For added conversational fluency practice, each *Listening* section ends with an "Ask & Answer" discussion task.

- Language Focus sections. These sections focus on essential grammar points and provide opportunity for fluency practice through a wide variety of activity types, from more controlled exercises to more personalized, free-response type activities and open-ended communication tasks such as role plays or interviews.

- Speaking sections. Each of these sections presents a specific speaking skill or strategy and outlines a communicative activity that helps you to develop your fluency by providing opportunities for you to use new language and vocabulary items in a natural way.

- Writing sections. Each of these sections in *World Pass* provides instruction and practice with different kinds of writing such as business and personal letters, summarizing information, and persuasive writing.

- Communication sections. The *Communication* sections that conclude each main unit consolidate and review the language material presented in the unit. Communication tasks vary widely and contribute to the development of fluency by focusing on meaningful speaking practice in activities such as games, presentations, interviews, and discussions.

- Expansion Pages. Each unit of *World Pass* is followed by *Expansion Pages*. The *Expansion Pages* are designed for students who want to learn additional vocabulary on their own and to have additional practice with the words and expressions presented in the units. Because the *Expansion Pages* are meant for self-study, they consist of exercises that you can do independently and then check your own answers.

SOME LANGUAGE LEARNING TIPS

Becoming a fluent speaker of English can be challenging, but it can also be a highly rewarding experience. Here are a few tips to help you make the most of the experience.

To increase your vocabulary:
- **Keep a vocabulary log.** Keep a list of new vocabulary items in the back pages of a notebook. From time to time, count up the number of words you have learned. You will be surprised at how quickly the number increases.
- **Use new words in sentences.** To fix news words in your mind, put them into sentences of your own. Do the maximum, not the minimum, with new vocabulary.
- **Make flashcards.** Create vocabulary flashcards that allow you to categorize, label, personalize, and apply new words. Put the words and their definitions on individual cards. Include a sample sentence that shows how the word is used in context.

To improve your speaking skills:
- **Read aloud.** Reading examples and texts out loud is a way of gaining confidence in speaking and letting the patterns of English "sound in your head." Even speaking out loud to yourself can be good practice.
- **Record yourself speaking.** Try recording yourself whenever you can. When you listen to the recording afterwards, don't worry if you sound hesitant or have made mistakes. If you do this several times, you will find that each version is better than the last.

To improve your reading skills:
- **Read passages more than once.** Reading the same reading passage several times will help you increase your reading speed and improve your fluency.
- **Summarize what you read.** When you summarize, you tell the main facts or ideas without giving all the details. Summarizing is a good way to be sure you really understand what you have read.

To improve your writing skills:
- **Increase the amount of writing you do.** For example, you might keep a personal diary in English, write small memos to yourself, or write a summary of a reading passage. The more you write, the more fluent and error-free your writing will become.
- **Analyze different types of writing.** Look at examples of different types of writing you may want to do: essays, formal letters, e-mail messages. Notice the form of the writing and think about what you could imitate to increase your fluency in writing.

To improve your listening comprehension:
- **Listen to recorded material several times.** You aren't expected to understand everything the first time your hear it. If you listen several times, you will probably understand something new each time.
- **Predict what you will hear.** Try to guess what you will hear before you listen. This will help you to focus while you listen and understand more of what you hear.

As you complete each unit of *World Pass*, ask yourself the questions on the **Learning Tips Checklist** below to keep track of the tips you are using and to remind yourself to try using others. To become a truly fluent speaker of English, you will need to practice the different language skills in a variety of ways. Find out what ways work best for you and use them to your advantage.

Sincerely,
Susan Stempleski

Learning Tips Checklist
Which language learning tips did you use as you worked through the unit? Note the ones you used and think about which were most helpful. As you work through the next unit, continue using the helpful ones and try using ones you haven't yet implemented.

Did you . . .

- ❏ record new words in a vocabulary log?
- ❏ try using new words in sentences?
- ❏ make and use vocabulary flashcards?
- ❏ read aloud as often as you could?
- ❏ record and listen to yourself speaking?
- ❏ read reading passages more than once?
- ❏ summarize what you read?
- ❏ write a lot and frequently?
- ❏ analyze and imitate different types of writing?
- ❏ listen to recorded material several times?
- ❏ predict what you would hear before you listened?

World Pass Upper-Intermediate

Scope and Sequence

What's the Story?

Lesson A | The story of my life

1 VOCABULARY FOCUS

What's the story?

People use the word *story* in many different ways, for example, a *news story* or a *bedtime story*. What are some other ways people use *story*? Make a list and tell the class.

A Read these four short conversations. Who do you think might have these conversations? Where might the people be?

1. A: What's his <u>story</u>?
   B: He says he was at home watching TV when the robbery occurred.

2. A: I don't want to hear any more <u>stories</u> out of you, young man!
   B: But it's true! I didn't eat all the cookies. I swear!

3. A: What's the magazine's cover <u>story</u> this week?
   B: The Olympics. The Games are big news right now.

4. A: How was the movie?
   B: The special effects were excellent, but the <u>story</u> was too predictable.

B Pair work. Look at the conversations in A. How is the word *story* used in each one? Match each use with its definition.

_____ an article or report in a newspaper or magazine

_____ the events in a book, movie, or person's life

_____ an alibi

_____ a fabricated description of events

C Pair work. Read what the three people in the pictures are saying. Pay attention to the words in blue.

> *We had two suspects. I believed the first guy. We could verify his story easily—all the facts made sense. The second guy was completely inconsistent and was always altering his story. All the facts were conflicting. You can usually tell when someone is making up a story. It just doesn't seem real.*

> *I could go after a lot of stories. There are many choices, but I have to pick one. Personally, I like to cover the stories about politics. Of course, before a story is published, I have to go over it and make sure the facts are accurate. That part of the job is boring.*

> *People interpret my short stories in different ways. Everyone has their own opinion about what they mean. My stories are complex. You have to piece together the story and figure out who you think the criminal is.*

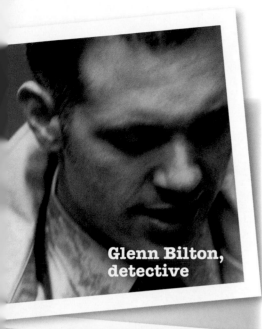

**Glenn Bilton,
detective**

**Cassandra Chu,
news reporter**

**Patricia Adams,
mystery author**

D   Place the verbs in blue in C into the chart below.

Meaning	Verb
1. inventing something (to fool someone)	making up
2. review	
3. figure out what happened	
4. analyze (to get the meaning)	
5. changing	
6. report a news story	
7. pursue an idea	
8. check to see if something is true	

▶ **Ask & *Answer***

Have you ever made up a story? Have you ever told a white lie (an untrue story told to avoid hurting someone's feelings)?

≫≫ **Vocabulary Builder** ◢◣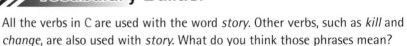

All the verbs in C are used with the word *story*. Other verbs, such as *kill* and *change*, are also used with *story*. What do you think those phrases mean? What other verbs can be used with *story*?

2 LISTENING

Everybody has a story.

A   Pair work. Al Benning, a professor in the anthropology department at UCLA, is doing a community research project called "Everybody Has a Story." What do you think it's about? Tell your partner.

EVERYBODY
HAS A STORY.

B Pair work. Listen. Take notes and then answer these questions with a partner. (CD Track 01)

1. What is the "Everybody Has a Story" booth and how does it work?

_____

_____

2. What is the story booth's purpose?

_____

_____

C Listen again to Mary's story only. Complete the chart. (CD Track 02)

1. Year she started working in café	
2. What she did in the café in the 50s	
3. What she wasn't allowed to do	
4. What she does in the café now	

▶ **Ask & Answer**

Why is Mary's personal story important?
What historical information does it give us?

3 LANGUAGE FOCUS
Review of the simple past and present perfect

A Clive Edwards is a journalist. Read about his life and notice the highlighted verb forms. Then read the sentences below and circle the correct answers.

> My father worked as a journalist for over thirty years. He died ten years ago. I've also worked as a journalist for my entire career. It's a wonderful job. I worked for CNN in the 1990s, and now I work for The Sun Times. I've reported from countries in Asia, Africa, and South America. I've seen a lot of exciting situations. I just received my new assignment. They want to send me to Mexico City. I don't know if I'll accept it. I haven't decided yet.

1. The sentence "My father <u>worked</u> as a journalist . . ." tells us that Clive's father is still / no longer a journalist.
2. The sentence "<u>I've</u> also <u>worked</u> as a journalist . . ." tells us that Clive is still / no longer a journalist.
3. The sentence "I <u>worked</u> for CNN . . ." tells us about a specific point / non-specific time in Clive's work history.
4. The sentence "<u>I've reported</u> from countries . . ." tells us about a specific point / non-specific time in Clive's work history.
5. The sentence "<u>I've seen</u> a lot of exciting situations" tells us that Clive is talking about a repeated action / something that happened once in the indefinite past.
6. The sentence "I <u>haven't decided yet</u>," shows that the present perfect + *not yet* is used to talk about things that have not happened before now / happened at a specific time in the past.

B Read this radio interview with journalist Clive Edwards.
Write the simple past or present perfect form of the verb in parentheses.

Interviewer: Today's guest is Mr. Clive Edwards. He
_____ (1. graduate) summa cum laude
from Brown University in 1991. Today he is an
award-winning journalist for the XPTV Network. How
long _____ you _____ (2. work) as a
reporter?

Clive: More than fifteen years.

Int: Mr. Edwards, what _____ (3. be) your most
memorable experience to date?

CE: I _____ (4. go after) many stories in my career,
but the one about the international space station
_____ (5. be) the most memorable. In fact, I'm
still covering that story as it continues to develop.

Int: You _____ (6. visit) some dangerous places in
the 1990s.

CE: Yes, I did. I often _____ (7. go) to war zones.

Int: _____ you _____ (8. choose) where you
would be assigned?

CE: No. I just _____ (9. go) wherever I was told.

Int: _____ you ever _____ (10. feel)
scared on the job?

CE: Of course. Just last year a bomb _____
(11. explode) near me. That _____ (12. is)
terrifying.

Int: _____ you ever _____ (13. be)
injured?

CE: Fortunately, no. I'm happy to say I _____ never
_____ (14. be) hurt at all! It's amazing
considering some of the things I've done to get a story!

Int: Yesterday you _____ (15. win) the "Courage in
Journalism" award. Congratulations!

CE: Thanks.

C Pair work. Act out the role play.

Student A: Imagine you are a famous person from
one of the following fields.
Tell your partner your name.

Student B: You are a journalist interviewing a famous
person. Think of three or four questions to ask your
famous partner and conduct an interview.

| entertainment | sports |
| politics | other: _____ |

How long have you . . . ?
When did you first . . . ?
What has been your most memorable . . . ?
Have you ever . . . ?

D Pair work. Switch roles and do the role play again.

4 SPEAKING

Did I ever tell you about the time . . . ?

A Put the events of the story in order. Notice the expressions in blue that are used when telling a story.

a. ____ **It happened when** we were living in an old house on Beach Street. Everyone in the neighborhood said it was haunted, but we just laughed and ignored them.

b. ____ I was shocked at what I saw! The living room furniture was in different positions! My wife immediately said, "A ghost moved our furniture!" Then we heard a noise from the closet. **In the end,** it wasn't a ghost after all. We opened the door and saw my cousin hiding there. He was playing a joke on us.

c. ____ **Did I ever tell you about the time** there was a ghost in our house?

d. ____ **It seems funny now, but** at the time we were really scared!

e. ____ **One night** however, we were asleep in our bedrooms upstairs. **Suddenly,** we heard some loud thumping noises downstairs. At first, I was too sleepy to do anything about it. But finally, I went downstairs to investigate.

An ogre fights a dragon with the help of a talking donkey and then marries a beautiful princess? Old news! The storyline from the hit movie *Shrek* is exciting, but nothing new. A hero facing a challenge, meeting a magical helper, and being rewarded are all examples of "universal themes"—story concepts that can be found almost anywhere in the world!

B Write each expression from A under an appropriate category in the chart below.

Introducing the story	Giving general background information	
I'll never forget the time . . .	A couple of years ago . . .	_____
<u>Did I ever tell you about the time</u> . . .	Last summer . . .	_____

Introducing the action	Ending the story	Reflecting back on the story
All of a sudden . . . _____	What happened in the end was . . . _____	Looking back on it, . . . _____

C Pair work. Think of a time when one of these things happened. Then tell your partner a story about it. Use the expressions from B.

- You saw something scary.
- You lost something important.
- You did something very embarrassing/funny/risky.
- Your idea: _____

> *I'll never forget the time I lost my house keys. It was a couple of years ago . . .*

Listening to a story

Showing you're listening:
Wow!   *Are you kidding?*
Really!   *Are you joking?*
Unbelievable!

Asking follow-up questions:
And then what happened?
What did you do next?

Interrupting to clarify:
Do you mean?
Did you say?

What's the Story?

| *Lesson B* | Tell me a story. |

1 GET READY TO READ

The moral of the story

Do you have a favorite story? What is it?
What is it about? Does it teach a lesson?

A **Pair work. Read this excerpt from Amy Tan's book** *The Joy Luck Club.*
Then answer the questions below with a partner.

1. What's the moral of this story?
2. Do you agree with this lesson? Why or why not?
3. Have you ever done something that you were warned not to do?
   What happened?

"Do not ride your bicycle around the corner," the mother
had told her daughter when she was seven.

"Why not!" protested the girl.

"Because then I cannot see you and you will fall down and
cry and I will not hear you."

"How do you know I'll fall?" whined the girl.

"It is in a book, *The Twenty-Six Malignant Gates*, all the
bad things that can happen to you outside the protection of
this house."

"I don't believe you. Let me see the book."

"It is written in Chinese. You cannot understand it. That is
why you must listen to me."

"What are they, then?" the girl demanded. Tell me the
twenty-six bad things."

But the mother sat knitting in silence.

"What twenty-six!" shouted the girl.

The mother still did not answer her.

"You can't tell me because you don't know! You don't
know anything!" And the girl ran outside, jumped on her
bicycle, and in her hurry to get away, she fell before she even
reached the corner.

B **Pair work. The words and phrases below are all in the reading on page 9. What do you think the story
excerpt is going to be about? Tell your partner. Then read the story excerpt and see if your ideas were correct.**

| stormy night | family | visitor | magic charm | wish | fate |

A   Read the excerpt from the story "The Monkey's Paw" on page 9.
Then number the events from the story in the correct order.

____   Mr. White uses the monkey's paw to make a wish.
____   Mr. and Mrs. White receive some money.
_1_   Sergeant-Major Morris returns from traveling overseas.
____   Herbert goes to work.
____   Morris visits the White family and shows them a monkey's paw.
____   Morris tries to destroy the monkey's paw.
____   A man from Maw and Meggins comes to visit Mr. and Mrs. White.

B   Read the story excerpt again. Then complete the sentences by circling the correct answer.

1. The word *expectantly* in line 5 means with anger / in anticipation.
2. The word *sorry* in line 31 means in trouble / embarrassed.
3. The word *solemnly* in line 46 means very cheerfully / seriously.
4. The word *consequences* in line 54 means bad or harmful results / positive or exciting results.
5. The phrase *your loss* in line 83 refers to the death of a loved one / something misplaced.

C   Pair work. Answer these questions on a separate piece of paper. Then check your answers with a partner.

1. How does Sergeant-Major Morris feel about the monkey's paw?
   What does Herbert think of it? Explain your answers.
2. A man from the factory comes to visit the Whites. How does he feel?
   Why does he feel this way?
3. What is surprising about the end of the story excerpt?

> ### Inferencing
>
> Information is not always stated directly. Often a reader must infer, or make guesses about something, using information that is available in the reading.

▶ ***Ask & Answer***
What is the moral of this story? Explain your answer.
If you were given three wishes, what would you ask for?
How would your life be better? How might it be worse?

The Monkey's Paw

Adapted from a story by W. W. Jacobs

Outside, it was a stormy night, but in the White's small living room, the fire burned brightly. Mr. White and his son, Herbert, were playing a game of chess when there was a knock at the door.

"There he is," said Herbert expectantly, rising with his father.

Moments later, Mr. White entered the room, followed by a tall, heavy-set man.

"Sergeant-Major Morris," White said, introducing his friend.

The middle-aged soldier shook hands with Mrs. White and Herbert. He then chose a comfortable chair by the fire while Mr. White prepared drinks. After his third drink, Morris's eyes got brighter, and he began to tell stories of distant countries. The family listened with interest.

"I'd like to travel myself," said White. "Say… what was that you were telling me the other day about a monkey's paw from India, Morris?"

"Nothing," said the soldier quickly. "Anyway, nothing worth hearing."

"Monkey's paw?" said Mrs. White curiously.

"Well," said the sergeant-major, "I guess you could say it's a kind of magic charm…"

Morris took the paw out of his pocket and held it up. Mrs. White moved back and frowned; Herbert took it and examined it curiously.

"What's so special about it?" asked Mr. White.

"A holy man in India believed that fate controls our lives. He thought that those who tried to change their fate would be sorry. He put a spell on the paw so that three separate men could each have three wishes."

"And have you had your three wishes?" asked Herbert smiling playfully.

"I have," said the soldier quietly. His face turned white.

"And has anybody else wished?" asked Mrs. White.

"The first man had his three wishes, yes. I don't know what the first two were, but the third was for death. That's how I got the paw."

The group fell silent.

Suddenly Morris took the paw and threw it in the fire. Mr. White, with a cry, picked it up.

"Let it burn," said the soldier solemnly.

"If you don't want it, Morris, let me keep it," said Mr. White.

"I won't. I threw it on the fire. Throw it back."

White shook his head and looked closely at the paw. "How do you make a wish?" he asked.

Morris sighed. "Hold it in your right hand and wish aloud," he said, "but I'm warning you—there will be consequences."

"I don't know what to wish for," said White.

"Wish for two hundred pounds, father," suggested Herbert. He winked at his mother.

His father held up the paw. "I wish for two hundred pounds."

Suddenly, White cried out. "It moved! As I made the wish, the paw moved in my hands like a snake!"

"Now dear…" said his wife.

"Well father," said Herbert laughing, "I don't see any money, and I bet I never will."

"Very funny," replied White, now calmer. "Still, it scared me all the same."

"I'm sure that Herbert will have some more of his jokes about that monkey's paw when he comes home from work tonight," said Mrs. White, as she and her husband were eating dinner the next evening.

"I'm sure he will," replied Mr. White, "but I'll say it again, the thing moved in my hand."

His wife didn't answer. She was watching a man outside the house. She noticed that the stranger was well dressed. He paused at the gate. Mrs. White hurried to answer the door. She brought the stranger into the room. "I . . . I come from Maw and Meggins," he said nervously.

"The factory? Has something happened to Herbert?" asked Mrs. White, anxiously.

"I'm sorry. Your son was caught in the machinery," the visitor said quietly. "The firm wants me to tell you how sorry they are for your loss," he said. "They wish to give you this check . . ."

Mr. White stood up and looked in horror at his visitor. "How much?"

"Two hundred pounds, Sir . . ."

3 WRITING
Chronological order

A **Pair work. Read the story. Then answer the questions with a partner.**

1. What "mistake" is the author writing about?
2. Why was this a mistake? What went wrong?
3. What is the author's advice to the reader?

Using time expressions and phrases

List events in chronological order to show when they happened. One way to make the sequence of events clear in a story is to use time expressions and phrases such as the ones below.

First of all,	*Next,*	*Then,*
Two months later,	*Before,*	*After,*
Finally,	*Later,*	

One of the biggest mistakes I've ever made was buying a car. I always wanted a car and thought that having one would make my life easier. I still remember the day I bought the car—my car!—and drove it home. It was the happiest day of my life . . . and then everything went wrong.

First of all, I got a ticket for speeding. I was so excited about driving my new car that I didn't realize how fast I was going. Later, when I got home, there was nowhere to park on the street. I looked for parking for almost thirty minutes. Finally, I found a place—six blocks from my house! The next morning, I decided to drive to school. The traffic was terrible and I was fifteen minutes late for class. All this happened in the first twenty-four hours of owning a car! By the end of the first year, I was almost $2,000 in debt. I needed money for car payments, gas, and insurance. It was crazy! In the end, I had to sell the car to pay my bills.

So what's the moral of the story? If you don't need a car, don't buy one. They are an expensive headache!

B Read the story again and underline the words and phrases used to show the order in which the events happened. The first one has been done for you.

C Think of something you did in your life—something that turned out differently than you expected. List the sequence of events below.

D Use your outline from C and time expressions to write a paragraph about your experience.

E Pair work. Exchange your paper with a partner. Notice the time expressions your partner uses. Is the sequence of events clear? Ask your partner questions about his or her story.

Something you thought would be great:　*Example:* buying a dog

- First, _____
- _____
- _____
- _____
- _____

Activity 1: What's *your* story?

A Imagine that Al Benning (from Listening, page 3) has set up a story booth in your city. You're at the booth with your partner. Read the interview questions below and add two of your own.

Everybody Has a Story

1. Please tell me your name and where you were born.

2. What was it like growing up in _____ [*your city*]? What were some of your favorite places? Have those places changed?

3. What did you want to be when you were a kid?

4. Who were your heroes or role models growing up? Who did you look up to?

5. _____?

6. _____?

B Pair work. Use the questions above to interview your partner.
During the interview, ask additional questions to learn more details. Take notes.

C Group work. Review your notes. What's one new thing you learned about your partner? Tell the class.

Activity 2: The story continues

A Group work. Get into a group of three people. Look back at the end of "The Monkey's Paw" on page 9. Follow the steps below.

1. The story does not end with the Whites receiving the 200 pounds. What do you think happens next in the story? Discuss your ideas.
2. Based on your ideas, make up a dialog to end the story.
3. Practice acting out your dialog.

B Group work. Perform your role play for another group. Were your endings similar or different?

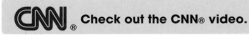 **Check out the CNN® video.** **Practice your English online at elt.heinle.com/worldpass**

Expansion Pages

A Match each expression containing *story* with its usage.

1. <u>To make a long story short</u>, I applied for the job, but I didn't get it. ___
2. I don't care if Laura gets angry with me. I'm not going to her party—<u>end of story</u>. ___
3. <u>It's the same old story</u>. I went on a diet, I lost ten pounds, and then I gained them all back, just like last time. ___
4. Patrick's office is neat and well-organized, but his apartment <u>is a different story</u>. ___
5. <u>What's the story?</u> You promised you'd be here two hours ago! ___

a. to show a contrast between two things, especially one that surprises you
b. to demand an explanation for something that you are unhappy about
c. to talk about something disappointing that has happened many times before
d. to summarize a sequence of events and avoid telling every detail
e. to put a stop to an argument and show that you don't want to discuss something anymore

B Fill in the blanks with one of the expressions from A.

1. I don't care what's on TV! You can't watch it until you've finished your homework. That's the rule—_____.
2. Just like always, I met a nice guy at work, we went out on a few dates, and then he never called me again. _____.
3. It rained every day, the hotel was terrible, there was a taxi drivers' strike so we couldn't go anywhere—_____, it was an awful vacation.
4. You told me you were going to buy groceries, but the fridge is empty. _____
5. My old boss was really nice and easygoing. My new boss _____—he's never satisfied with anything!

C Read about these different types of stories, and think of examples of each.
Then complete the sentences with one of the words in blue, adding articles (*a, an, the*) as needed.

A **tale** is a story about imaginary events, such as a fairy tale or a folktale. A **report** gives a detailed and objective presentation of facts, such as a newspaper report or a government report, while a **statement** is a short summary of facts. Speakers and writers like to use **anecdotes**, short stories about a real event, to illustrate and explain an idea. A **chronicle** is a long narrative of historical events told in time order. A **yarn** is a long entertaining story loosely based on the truth. Children enjoy **fables**, old stories about animals that teach a moral lesson. And too many people enjoy **gossip**—often untrue rumors about people.

1. Sarah's presentation had some interesting _____ about women who have started their own businesses.
2. In my country, we have a lot of old _____ about ghosts and princesses.
3. The government issued a brief _____ about the president's trip to Africa.
4. My grandfather loves to tell _____ about his adventures when he was in the navy. He exaggerates a lot, but they're really entertaining!
5. The Ministry of Environmental Protection released _____ on changes in water quality over the past ten years.
6. I don't believe that David is getting married. I think it's just _____.
7. Do you know _____ about the ant and the grasshopper?
8. This history book contains a detailed _____ of our country's struggle for independence.

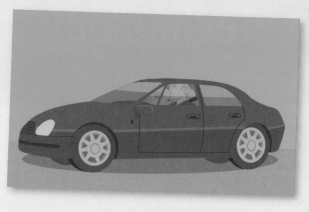

Incorrect: *I got on my car and drove to the office.*   **Correct:** *I got into my car and drove to the office.*

D Review the meaning of these words from "The Monkey's Paw" on page 9. Then use them to complete the sentences.

> fate (lines 29 & 31)   spell (line 31)   solemnly (line 46)
>
> expectantly (line 5)   consequences (line 54)   firm (line 82)

1. My grandmother really believes in _____. She thinks that we can't do anything to change what will happen to us in the future.
2. We waited _____ to find out the winner of the talent competition.
3. Infotek is a _____ that surveys consumers about their opinions on computer products.
4. At the president's funeral, thousands of people lined the streets of the capital and watched _____ as the car carrying his remains passed by.
5. If you cheat on an exam at our university, you face serious _____. You could receive a failing grade, or even be expelled from the university.
6. In the old story, the witch put a _____ on the three children and turned them into trees.

In Other Words

An **alibi** is proof that someone was not near a crime scene and therefore could not have committed the crime: *He is not a suspect because he has a good alibi; he was out of town visiting his sister on the night the robbery took place.*

An **excuse** is a reason given to explain a wrongdoing or offence: *He had a good excuse for being late for the meeting; his car broke down.*

An **explanation** is information given to help someone understand something: *The guide in the museum provided a very clear explanation of how the ancient pottery was made and used.*

A **moral** is the practical lesson in a fable: *The moral of "The Grasshopper and the Ant" is that we should always plan for the future.*

A **lesson** is something that you learn from an experience: *I learned many lessons from traveling alone.*
It's also a course of instruction that develops a skill: *Sarah is taking swimming lessons.*

A **message** is the most important idea in a book or movie: *The message of the movie* Titanic *is that love is stronger than death.*

tell and say
The verb *tell* is used with an object:
   I told my friend a joke / the truth / a story / a lie / the answer.
We use *say* when we report someone's words:
   I said, "You're late."
   He said he had missed the bus.

Technology

Lesson A | Technostress

1 VOCABULARY FOCUS
Information overload

WARM UP Many people today use IMs (instant messages) to communicate instantly over the Internet. What are some of the advantages and disadvantages of sending IMs?

A **Pair work. Categorize the phrases below. Can you add any more ideas to the list?**

adds stress to the workplace   distracts from regular work   fosters communication
speeds up decision-making   saves time   makes it easier to stay in touch

Advantages of sending IMs	Disadvantages of sending IMs

B **Read this letter to an advice columnist. What is Ms. Silva's problem? Notice the words in blue.**

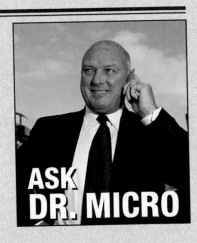

ASK DR. MICRO

Dear Dr. Micro,

I need your help. I am drowning in **information overload** at work. Between the telephone calls, voicemail systems, e-mail messages, and faxes, it's becoming too much. At the office I am often trying to carry on a conversation while typing a memo and checking the time for my next conference call.

I spend my days sitting in front of my computer or talking to clients on the telephone. I have almost no face-to-face **interaction** with people during the day. And at night, it's the same problem as I try to answer e-mail and IMs from my friends and family. I thought all this technology was supposed to make my life easier, but it's rapidly becoming a **recipe for disaster**. I feel chained to my computer.

—*Nadia Silva*

Dear Ms. Silva,

Technology can help us save time and money, but only if we use it wisely. There are some things you can do to help your situation—it isn't hopeless by any means.

1. Cut back on the **multitasking**: When you try to do more than one task at once, you lose focus and become less efficient.
2. Spend more time with family, coworkers, and friends: A computer is not a friend—it is an **impersonal** machine with its own limitations. Get out at night and take an exercise class or an art class—something you enjoy. Seeing other people **promotes** a sense of community and besides, it's fun!
3. Get some exercise: Sitting in front of a computer all day is a **sedentary** activity—you need to find something active to do. Why don't you take time at lunch for a brisk 20-minute walk with a coworker and get caught up on office gossip?

Heavy **dependence** on computers and other machines can be unhealthy. Follow the suggestions above, though, and you'll feel freer than you have in a long time. I tried them myself and found them to be **liberating** indeed. Good luck!

—*Dr. Micro*

C Locate the correct word or phrase in the article on page 14. Write your answers below.

Find a word or phrase that means:
1. doing more than one thing at once: _____
2. encourages: _____
3. having too much information to absorb: _____
4. reliance on: _____
5. inactive: _____
6. contact: _____
7. freeing: _____
8. distant: _____
9. will likely cause something bad to happen: _____

D Pair work. Which of the words or phrases in C can you associate with IMs?

>>> Vocabulary Builder ▲

A. The word *interaction* is often followed by the preposition *with*. Find the word *recipe* in the column. What preposition is it followed by? What other noun + preposition combinations do you know?

B. Circle the appropriate prepositions.
   1. What is the cure for / to "technostress?"
   2. I haven't had any dealings for / with their IT Department.
   3. Our dependence on / with technology is not always good.

2 LISTENING
When technology doesn't work

Talk about a time you had a problem with technology (for example, your cell phone didn't work). How did you feel? What did you do?

> **Real English**
> *get to the bottom of (something)* = find the truth or cause of a problem

A Listen to this news report. Then circle the correct answers below that describe the report. (CD Tracks 03 & 04)

This is a daytime / evening report on radio / TV about a blackout / storm that happened in the summer / winter.

> **Talking about cause and effect**
>
> Speakers use these phrases to link cause and effect:
>
> *. . . was the cause of . . .*
> *. . . was responsible for . . .*
> *As a result, . . .*

B Listen again. What caused these three things to happen? Write your answers. (CD Track 05)

CAUSE		EFFECT
1. [ ]	➤	no electricity
2. [ ]	➤	eleven deaths
3. [ ]	➤	extra police on the street

C Listen and complete these items with the appropriate number or numerical expression. (CD Track 06)

1. houses without power: _____
2. length of time with no electricity: _____
3. deaths: _____
4. recent temperatures: _____
5. cooling centers: _____
6. stores broken into: _____

> **Ask & Answer**
> Have you ever been in a blackout, a bad storm, an earthquake, or a similar event? What happened?

3 LANGUAGE FOCUS
Review of the passive voice

A Read the sentences. Notice the words in blue.

> The object of an active sentence becomes the subject of a passive sentence.
> Thomas Edison introduced the first phonograph in 1877.
> The first phonograph was introduced in 1877.
>
> Use the passive voice when . . .
> • you don't know who did something: Oh no! My bag has been stolen!
> • who did the action is not as important as what happened: Our product was tested using the most rigorous standards.
> • who did the action is obvious from the situation: My computer is being repaired today.
> • a general group of people do the action: New Year's Day is celebrated here on January 1.

B Pair work. Read these sentences. The passive voice is preferred in each one. Why? Choose a reason from the chart above. Discuss with a partner.

1. Cell phone usage isn't allowed in the library.
2. Bad news! My shipment is being held at the airport.
3. Has the recycling been picked up yet?
4. Was this product made in Malaysia?

C Read the ad about the Vesta, a hybrid car, on page 17. Then read these statements below. The statements are incorrect. Respond to each statement with the correct answer. Use the verbs in parentheses and the passive voice.

1. The Vesta uses a single kind of motor.
   No, it doesn't. It's powered by a traditional engine and an electric motor. (power)

2. It's a Japanese car.
   _____ (manufacture)

3. You can only buy it in Canada right now.
   _____ (sell)

4. You can buy it in Europe this week.
   _____ (introduce)

5. Critics don't like it.
   _____ (vote)

6. It's too expensive for the average consumer.
   _____ (purchase)

16   Unit 2 • Techonology

Introducing . . . **The Vesta . . .**
made in Canada

+ uses both a traditional engine and an electric motor to save energy
+ already available in the U.S. and Canada
+ available throughout Latin America and Asia this week

Students, doctors, actors, construction workers, artists, housewives . . . join the everyday ranks of Vesta owners! You can afford it!

New Model Magazine voted the Vesta "best new car this year."

D Pair work. Look at the technological achievements to the right. Then ask and answer the questions below with a partner. Use your own ideas to complete the statements. Then make original sentences.

Satellite dish

- Why was . . . invented?
    It was invented so that . . .
    It was invented in order to . . .

- How has the world been changed by this invention?
    The world has become . . .
    Photos can be sent . . .
    TV shows can be watched . . .

E Pair work. What invention in the past fifty years has made the biggest impact on society? Decide on your answer. Take notes on your reasons. Tell the class.

World Link

Digital camera

OPTICAL 2x
6x
2.0 MEGA PIXELS
f = 6.3-12.6mm 1:3.8
MULTI POINT AF

A Pair work. Read about the situation below. Pay attention to the
words in blue. Who should Jim go to for help? Why?

Saying you're able or not able to do something

Jim's computer has crashed and he doesn't know what to do.
Read what these different people said to Jim.

Paolo: I might be able to help you. I know something
about computers.

Kim: Let me look at it. I'm pretty good at fixing
things.

Jesse: What should you do? I haven't got a clue about
it. Ask Emi.

Emi: I know something about computers. I'm busy
now, but I can help you later.

Jacques: I'm sorry, but I'm no good at fixing things,
especially computers.

Gloria: I don't have the faintest idea how to fix it. Call
a repair service.

B Read the statements below. What do you notice
about the words that follow the expressions in blue?

	Agree	Disagree
1. I might be able to change a tire if I had to.	☐	☐
2. I'm pretty good at typing on an English keyboard.	☐	☐
3. I'm pretty good at golf.	☐	☐
4. I haven't got a clue about scuba diving.	☐	☐
5. I know something about computers.	☐	☐
6. I'm no good at karaoke.	☐	☐
7. I'm no good at speaking in front of a group of people.	☐	☐
8. I don't have the faintest idea how to cook Italian food.	☐	☐

C Pair work. Read the statements in B again. Think about your own answers for each statement,
and check (✓) *Agree* or *Disagree*. Then explain your answers to a partner.

> *I might be able to change a tire if I had to.*
> *My dad showed me how to do it.*

> *Not me! I wouldn't know what to do!*

D Pair work. Is there something your partner knows how to do or is good at that you're not?
Ask your partner to explain how to do it.

Technology

Lesson B | Techno-shopping

1 GET READY TO READ

Shopping habits

WARM UP

Do you like shopping? Why or why not?
What do you like shopping for?
What do you hate shopping for?

A Pair work. **Complete the shopping survey below.
Then explain your answers to a partner.**

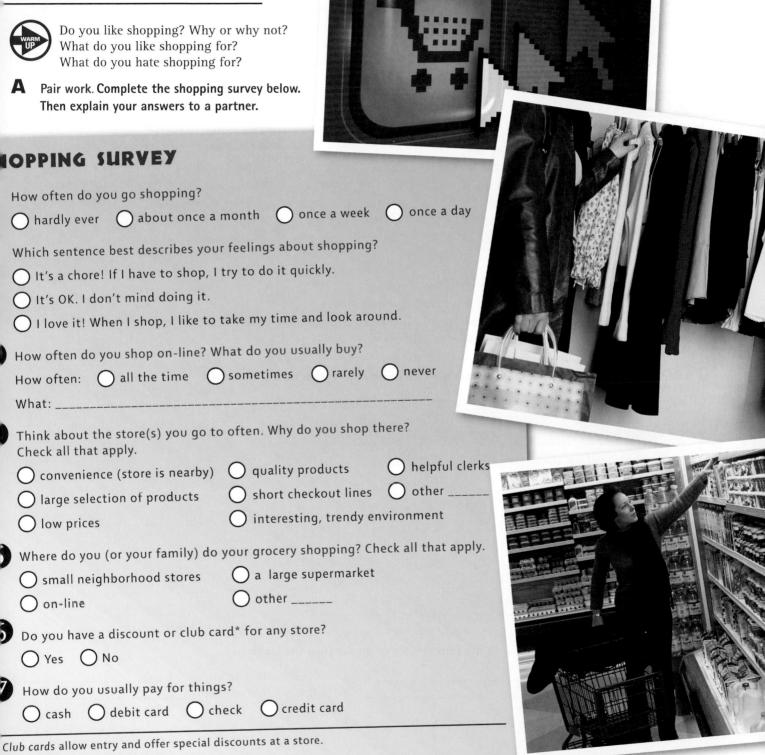

HOPPING SURVEY

How often do you go shopping?

○ hardly ever   ○ about once a month   ○ once a week   ○ once a day

Which sentence best describes your feelings about shopping?

○ It's a chore! If I have to shop, I try to do it quickly.

○ It's OK. I don't mind doing it.

○ I love it! When I shop, I like to take my time and look around.

How often do you shop on-line? What do you usually buy?

How often: ○ all the time   ○ sometimes   ○ rarely   ○ never

What: _____

Think about the store(s) you go to often. Why do you shop there?
Check all that apply.

○ convenience (store is nearby)   ○ quality products   ○ helpful clerks

○ large selection of products   ○ short checkout lines   ○ other _____

○ low prices   ○ interesting, trendy environment

Where do you (or your family) do your grocery shopping? Check all that apply.

○ small neighborhood stores   ○ a large supermarket

○ on-line   ○ other _____

Do you have a discount or club card* for any store?

○ Yes   ○ No

How do you usually pay for things?

○ cash   ○ debit card   ○ check   ○ credit card

Club cards allow entry and offer special discounts at a store.

B Pair work. The words in the left column are from the reading on page 21.
Match each one with the phrase in the right column that is most similar in
meaning. Then check your answers with a partner.

1. display (line 17) ____   a. a tool or piece of equipment
2. unique (line 25) ____   b. to implant something into something else
3. device (line 26) ____   c. to follow, to trace
4. automatically (line 36) ____ d. in danger, at risk
5. anonymously (line 38) ____   e. to show publicly
6. embed (line 41) ____   f. space to yourself so that others cannot see or hear what you're doing
7. track (line 46) ____   g. namelessly, in secret
8. privacy (line 46) ____   h. the only one of its kind, special
9. at stake (line 46) ____   i. done mechanically, without a person doing it
10. benefit (line 49) ____   j. an advantage

2 READING
Not Your Typical Store

A Skim the article quickly on page 21. Then write each
heading in the appropriate box in the reading.

How it works
But there are benefits, too . . .
~~A new way to shop~~
So, what's the problem?
A more convenient shopping experience

> Skimming a reading to get the main
> ideas quickly.
>
> When you skim, read the title, section
> headers, and the first sentence or two in
> each paragraph. Don't worry about words
> you don't know.

B Pair work. Read the article through line 20. How is the Extra Future Store different from most supermarkets?
Find three examples. Explain your answers to a partner.

C Read the rest of the article and complete the chart with information from the reading.

Using RFID chips in stores	
Reasons for	**Reasons against**
Shoppers will be able to find items in a store more quickly.	

D Complete the sentences below with the correct word or phrase from the reading.

1. In line 17, *It* refers to _____.
2. In line 41, *them* refers to _____.
3. In line 51, *these* refers to _____.
4. In line 55, *that* refers to _____.

Not Your Typical Store

Brian Nguyen

A new way to shop

It's Tuesday afternoon, and I'm in Rheinburg, Germany (a city just north of Dusseldorf), visiting the Extra Future Store. Metro AG, the parent company of the store, is one of Germany's largest retailers and its "store of the future" is attracting a lot of attention these days—but not for its prices. Instead, people are coming from all over to experience a new way to shop.

The experience is less like shopping in a supermarket and more like playing some kind of high-tech game. It starts as I enter the store and choose a shopping cart. First, I swipe my store ID card through a computer on the cart's handle. The computer's screen comes on, a map of the store appears, and the journey begins.

As I shop, antennas around the store send information about different specials to the computer on my cart. Attracted by one of the ads, I select a jar of olives that are on sale. I hold up the jar to a computer nearby. It displays the price and also suggests that a certain type of Spanish cheese would be good with the olives. The map on my cart shows me where to find the cheese. It's like the store is helping me to shop.

How does the Extra Future Store make this kind of shopping experience possible? The answer is *radio frequency identification chips* (or RFID, for short). Invented in 1969, RFID chips are about the size of a grain of sand. Each chip has a unique ID number and is attached to a product (e.g., a bottle of olives). Using a wireless device called an "RFID reader," one can get information from a chip about a product—for example, its price and location.

This type of technology could mean a more convenient experiece for shoppers. RFID chips will help shoppers find items in a store more quickly—products that are just right for them. In addition, people won't have to wait in long checkout lines to pay. In the supermarket of the future, you will simply walk through a checkout lane. The REID-tagged items in your cart will be read by a scanner, and your credit or debit card will be charged automatically.

Sounds good, right? Not to consumer activist Jeremy Webber. "Right now, I can buy something anonymously, especially if I pay with cash," says Webber. "But today, RFID chips are being put on product packaging. And a growing number of manufacturers are planning to embed them directly into products." (A chip will be sewn into a pair of shoes, for example, or be built into a shampoo bottle.)

"What this means," explains Webber, "is that if the RFID chip isn't disabled before you leave the store, your location could be tracked with an RFID reader. People's privacy is at stake."

Megan Lim, a store manager in Australia, believes that Webber's concerns are unnecessary. "Look, there are risks with every kind of new technology. But what about the benefits? If a store uses the chips, it can track which items are popular, and quickly order more of these. Stores can save money by ordering fewer of the less popular items. If the store saves money, then maybe shoppers will pay less for products, too." Lim pauses. "I think a lot of people will be willing to give up some of their privacy for that."

▶ **Ask & Answer**

Would you shop at a place like the Extra Future Store? Why or why not?

A Pair work. In this unit, you read about ways that RFID chips are being used in stores. Read and complete the paragraphs below using the phrases in the box. Then discuss the questions below with a partner.

> There are also disadvantages   Another drawback   Another benefit
> The downside to this   One advantage is that

Using RFID chips in stores has advantages and disadvantages. (1.) _____ shoppers will be able to find items in a store more quickly. A person won't need to wander up and down store aisles looking for products. (2.) _____ is that shoppers won't have to spend time standing in long checkout lines. They will simply walk through a checkout station, and their credit or debit card will be automatically billed.

(3.) _____ to using RFID chips in stores, though. As was noted, one of the pluses of using the chips is that a person's account will be automatically billed. (4.) _____, of course, is that a person will need a credit or debit card in order to buy things. (5.) _____ to using RFID chips relates to privacy. Unless a chip is disabled before a shopper leaves the store, his or her location can be tracked.

- How many advantages and disadvantages are discussed in each paragraph?
- Can you think of one more advantage and disadvantage? How would you add these to the paragraphs above?

B Pair work. Read the ad. With a partner, think of two reasons for and two reasons against using RFID chips on people.

> ## Call People Trackers Now!
>
> Our company has designed an RFID chip for people. The device is embedded under a person's skin. You can use it to track:
>
> your spouse, boyfriend or girlfriend, your children, or your employees!
>
> For more information, call (800) 555-TRAK today

Advantages	Disadvantages
1.	1.
2.	2.

C On a separate piece of paper, write a paragraph describing the pros and cons of using RFID chips with people. Use your ideas from B and the phrases from A in your paragraph.

D Pair work. Exchange your paragraph with a new partner. Notice the phrases your partner uses to describe the advantages and disadvantages.

Activity 1: Technology now and then

A Pair work. How much do you know about technology? Read and discuss the questions with a partner. Try to choose the correct answer for each.

B Group work. Join another pair.

- Compare your answers. Each correct answer is worth 10 points.
- The pair with the most points wins.

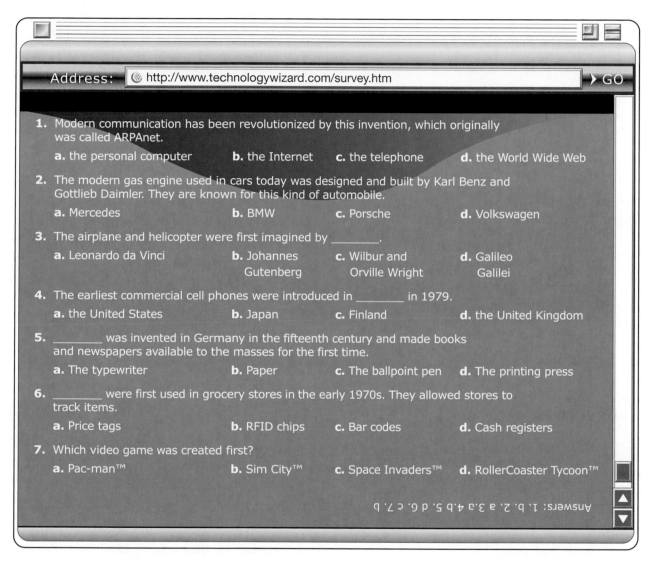

Address: http://www.technologywizard.com/survey.htm ▸ GO

1. Modern communication has been revolutionized by this invention, which originally was called ARPAnet.

   a. the personal computer   **b.** the Internet   **c.** the telephone   **d.** the World Wide Web

2. The modern gas engine used in cars today was designed and built by Karl Benz and Gottlieb Daimler. They are known for this kind of automobile.

   a. Mercedes   **b.** BMW   **c.** Porsche   **d.** Volkswagen

3. The airplane and helicopter were first imagined by _____.

   a. Leonardo da Vinci   **b.** Johannes Gutenberg   **c.** Wilbur and Orville Wright   **d.** Galileo Galilei

4. The earliest commercial cell phones were introduced in _____ in 1979.

   a. the United States   **b.** Japan   **c.** Finland   **d.** the United Kingdom

5. _____ was invented in Germany in the fifteenth century and made books and newspapers available to the masses for the first time.

   a. The typewriter   **b.** Paper   **c.** The ballpoint pen   **d.** The printing press

6. _____ were first used in grocery stores in the early 1970s. They allowed stores to track items.

   a. Price tags   **b.** RFID chips   **c.** Bar codes   **d.** Cash registers

7. Which video game was created first?

   a. Pac-man™   **b.** Sim City™   **c.** Space Invaders™   **d.** RollerCoaster Tycoon™

Answers: 1. b, 2. a 3. a 4. b 5. d 6. c 7. b

Activity 2: The pros and cons

A Pair work. Think of a simple problem in daily life that could be solved with the right technology. What is the problem? What could you invent to solve it?

1. Discuss your ideas.
2. Make a simple drawing of your invention.

B Group work. Take turns presenting your inventions to the rest of the class.

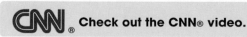 **Check out the CNN® video.** **Practice your English online at** elt.heinle.com/worldpass

Unit 2: Technology

A Some words are frequently used together in a phrase. Read this paragraph and underline the phrases with *trend*.

> Young people in many countries are <u>setting the trend</u> for a new pattern in telecommunication. There is a trend toward having only a cell phone as a replacement for a landline. Experts predict that the current trend will spread to developing countries, and the upward trend in the number of cell phone subscribers will continue for years to come. Analysts theorize that only a few countries will buck the trend and continue to add landlines instead.

B Study the phrases in the box and then complete the sentences with the phrases.

> **Word combinations with *trend***
>
> set(ting) the trend
> the latest/recent/current trend
> downward/upward trend
> reverse/buck the trend
>
> a trend toward having/buying/making (verb + *ing*)
> a trend in communication/fashion/music (noun)
> economic/social trends

1. In my country, there's _____ getting married at a later age. Nowadays people are waiting until they're 27 or 28.
2. More and more children are overweight. The government is hoping to _____ with nutrition programs and fitness classes in schools.
3. Fewer people every year are using fax machines. This _____ began about ten years ago with the popularity of e-mail.
4. *The Future of Money* is a new book about _____ in the world today.
5. Japanese companies are _____ for energy-efficient hybrid cars.

> **I didn't know that!**
> The English word *robot* comes from a Czech word which means "worker." In 1923, a Czech science fiction writer named Karl Capek wrote a book in which machines take over the world and embed circuits in people's brains to make them work like machines. He called these people *robots*.

C Review the meanings of the underlined terms from the reading on page 21. Then match the sentence parts.

1. I use my <u>debit card</u> ___.
2. I took a <u>shopping cart</u> ___.
3. The <u>checkout lines</u> are very long ___.
4. I have a <u>club card</u> ___.
5. I complained to the <u>manager</u> ___.
6. A special <u>scanner</u> shows you ___.
7. The <u>shelves</u> at the electronics store were empty ___.

a. because I planned to buy a lot of heavy things.
b. after the holiday sale ended.
c. when the store is busy.
d. because a store employee was very rude to me last time.
e. the price and other information about the product.
f. to pay for groceries, gasoline, and things I buy every day.
g. for the music store, so every time I buy ten CDs, I get one free.

Expansion Pages

D The prefix *over-* (meaning "too much") is used with certain nouns, verbs, and adjectives. Match the words with their meanings.

1. overdo it ___
2. overload ___
3. overlook ___
4. overpowering ___
5. overeat ___
6. overdue ___

a. unpleasantly strong
b. not done by the time required
c. give someone too much work or information
d. not notice something
e. eat too much
f. work too hard

E Now complete the sentences with the correct form of the terms in D.

1. Be careful not to _____! You just got out of the hospital!
2. All of my bills were _____ last month because I forgot to mail the payments.
3. On holidays, many people tend to _____ at family dinners and company parties.
4. My sister loves to wear perfume, but she uses so much that the scent is almost _____.
5. I had to rewrite my paper for English class. I _____ a lot of spelling mistakes, and my teacher made me correct them.
6. I'm _____ with e-mail messages—I get almost 100 of them every day.

In Other Words

Device is a general word for a machine with a special purpose: *They invented a new device for copying DVDs.*

An **appliance** is an electrical machine used in the household: *We got all new kitchen appliances, including a stove, fridge, and microwave oven.*

Gadget is an informal word for a small, clever tool: *I bought a gadget that keeps my coffee cup hot on my desk.*

Contraption is a humorous word for a funny-looking machine: *I don't think that contraption will really clean my bathroom automatically.*

Unique means being the only one like this in the world: *The architecture of the Sydney Opera Hall is truly unique.*

One of a kind is an informal expression: *Irina's dress is one of a kind. She made it herself.*

Without equal means better than any other: *The author's knowledge of world history is without equal.*

Special is sometimes used as an informal word for unique: *That photo of my family was a very special gift. Thanks so much!*

Watch out!

unique
Unique is an absolute term and does not have a comparative or superlative form. So you can't say "more unique" or "the most unique." Other words like this are *perfect* and *impossible.*

1 VOCABULARY FOCUS

She's a real go-getter.

 What are some characteristics that make someone a good employee?

A Intek Games is looking for a lead designer for their video games division. Read the adjectives below. Then add two that you think are important to the job description on the right.

thorough	motivated	creative
productive	energetic	sincere

B Here are two candidates for the job. Read about each person and notice the words in blue.

Wanted: Lead designer for video games division

- minimum five years experience in the gaming industry
- strong communication and leadership skills
- must be organized
- _____
- _____

Raphael has worked for Intek for six years. He's an early riser, a morning person, and, as a rule, gets to work by 7:00 before anyone else. He works well with other employees and likes collaborating on projects. On the whole, people think of him as a real team player. Even though he's got a great attitude, he can be a hothead under pressure and often loses his temper when there is a deadline. He also ends up doing extra work because he has difficulty saying no when people ask him to do something—even if it isn't his job. This gives him a reputation of being a pushover, although some say it means he's a hard worker who gives 100% to get the project done.

Damita has worked for Intek for five years. She's a real go-getter—a very ambitious employee. She was hired as the receptionist, took some classes, and has worked her way up quickly to be part of the design team. Not only is she a self-starter, she's a real risk taker. She likes to try new ways of doing things, even if it means making mistakes sometimes. Typically, she works a lot harder than she has to. Some of her colleagues say she's an overachiever. She is also a bit of a control freak. She has to have things done her way and often tries to manage even the smallest details of a project. It's very important to her to do a good job, but her colleagues think she tries to do it all and doesn't give them a chance to get their work done at their own pace.

C Pair work. Read the sentences. Who does each one describe?
Circle the correct answer. Then compare your answers with a partner.

This person . . .

1.	gets up early.	Raphael	Damita
2.	gets angry easily.	Raphael	Damita
3.	is easily controlled by others.	Raphael	Damita
4.	is a very ambitious person.	Raphael	Damita
5.	likes to give orders.	Raphael	Damita
6.	tries to cooperate with other people.	Raphael	Damita
7.	likes to try new things and isn't afraid of danger.	Raphael	Damita
8.	works harder than necessary to succeed.	Raphael	Damita

>>> Vocabulary Builder ▲

Look at these compound nouns and discuss the questions with a partner.

team player   go-getter   overachiever

1. What do you think these words mean?
2. What do you notice about how these words are written?
3. Find other words in the description of Raphael and Damita in A that are formed the same way.

▶ **Ask & Answer**
Which person would you choose for the job—Raphael or Damita? Why?

2 LISTENING
Opposites attract.

A Look at the photos of Sandra and Ali and then at the words below. Predict which words could be used to describe each of them.

homebody   free spirit
heartbreaker   night owl
early riser

Sandra

Ali

B Listen to Ali talk about a problem he's having with Sandra. What is the problem?
Write your answer below. (CD Tracks 07 & 08)

_____

_____

C Listen and write down the key words that describe each personality type.
Then circle the person each describes. (CD Track 09)

Personality type	Key words	Name	
1. a homebody	stays at home	Ali	Sandra
2. a free spirit		Ali	Sandra
3. a heartbreaker		Ali	Sandra
4. a night owl		Ali	Sandra

▶ **Ask & Answer**
Which of the words in A describe you or someone you know? In what other situations do people have to compromise to make things work?

3 LANGUAGE FOCUS

Adverb clauses of contrast, purpose, and time

Adverb Clauses

An adverb clause tells why, when, how, or where something happened. It modifies the verb or the main clause in a sentence.

A Read these sentences. Underline the adverb clause in each sentence.
Circle the word or phrase that introduces the clause.
Then answer the questions that follow.

> Set 1   a. I left the party early (because) I wasn't feeling well.
> b. I studied Italian so that I could communicate with my relatives.
> c. Since the movie doesn't start until 9:00, why don't we have dinner now?
>
> Set 2   a. I jumped when I heard a loud noise.
> b. Whenever I'm at home, I like to relax and just do nothing.
>
> Set 3   a. Though it was hot and humid, I didn't mind.
> b. I look a lot like my father, although he doesn't wear glasses and I do.

Which set of sentences contains adverb clauses that express:
a. a reason or purpose for doing something? _____
b. opposition or contrast? _____
c. time? _____

Real English
You can use *even though* instead of *although* or *though* with no change in meaning.

B Circle the correct word or phrase to complete each sentence.

1. (Even though / Because) I'm a morning person, I often arrive at school by 7:00 A.M.
2. (Since / Though) everyone's opinion is important, I consult with others before I make a big decision.
3. I get angry (whenever / even though) I make a mistake.
4. I like to supervise projects (although / so that) everything runs smoothly.
5. (Even though / Since) I don't consider myself ambitious, it's true that I never give up.
6. You have to take risks (since / though) you only live once.
7. I don't like to be in charge (so that / because) no one listens to me.
8. (Although / Since) everyone tells me not to work so hard, I can't stop myself.

C Pair work. What kind of person do you think would say each
sentence in B? Which sentences might you say?

> I think an early riser would say the first sentence.

> I definitely wouldn't say it because I like to sleep late!

D Complete each sentence with a logical ending.
Compare your answers with a partner.

1. Even though it was raining and cold, we decided to _____.
2. Because he's an overachiever, he always _____.
3. Since our plane leaves at 7:00 A.M., why don't we _____?
4. Although he seems like a team player, _____.
5. She took some web design classes so that _____.
6. She exercises and eats well because she _____.

E Pair work. Complete these sentences with your own information. Then share your information with a partner.

1. I always take _____ whenever _____.
2. I hardly ever _____ because _____ _____.
3. I'm studying English so that _____ _____.
4. Although I didn't _____, _____ _____.

> I always take my laptop whenever I go on vacation. What about you?

F Pair work. Read the situation below. Look at the list of advantages and disadvantages and add one or two of your own ideas to each list. Then, create a role play in which you discuss the possibilities, and then decide what to do. Use adverb clauses in some of your responses.

Scott and Zach are roommates. Doug is looking for a room. Play the roles of Scott, who wants another roommate, and Zach, who doesn't.

Advantages of getting a roommate	Disadvantages of getting a roommate
The rent will be cheaper. Doug's a very neat person. He's an early-riser who's rarely home. _____ _____	The apartment will be more crowded. Doug has two cats. He's quiet, but his friends aren't. _____ _____

Scott: I think we should get a roommate. The rent will be cheaper.
Zach: I don't know. Even though we can save money, the apartment will be more crowded.
Scott: That's true, but think about the chores. Since Doug's a neat person, . . .

World Link

"Ketsuekigata," the study of blood types and personality, is so important in Japan that when Naoko Takeuchi wrote the character profiles for her hit cartoon series *Sailor Moon*, she included the characters' blood types along with their names, hobbies, and favorite foods. (In case you're wondering, *Sailor Moon* is a Type O.)

4 SPEAKING

In general, what do you like to do for fun?

A Look at the sentences in the box. Pay attention to the words in blue. Are the conversations about things that happen all of the time or most of the time?

> **Making general statements**
>
> What kind of music do you listen to?
> > **Generally speaking**, I prefer rock. I sometimes also listen to R&B.
>
> **In general**, what do you like to do for fun?
> > I enjoy listening to music and shopping.
>
> Where do you like to go out with your friends?
> > **For the most part**, I like to go to clubs.
>
> **Typically**, what do you do on the weekend?
> > I sleep late!
>
> What do you do when you face a difficult problem?
> > **As a rule**, I think it over first. If I can't solve the problem, I'll ask a friend for advice.
>
> How often do you study?
> > **Normally** I study every day after school.

B Pair work. Answer the questions.

1. How would you answer the questions in the box above?
2. Add three questions of your own. Practice with a partner.
3. Based on your partner's answers, what do you think his or her personality type is?

C Group work. Work with another pair. Take turns describing your partner's personality type. Use the phrases in the box in A to explain your conclusions.

> *Generally speaking, my partner is a free spirit. She likes to relax on the weekends, go clubbing, and have fun.*

D Pair work. Role-play the following situation. Before you begin, choose one of the personality types below, but don't tell your partner. During the role play, answer the questions based on the personality type you choose.

free spirit	hothead	overachiever	risk taker
go-getter	introvert	pushover	team player

Situation: You're at the airport. Your flight has been delayed for two hours. You talk with each other while you are waiting for your flight. Take turns asking each other questions about your jobs, your hobbies, how you spend your free time, and so on.

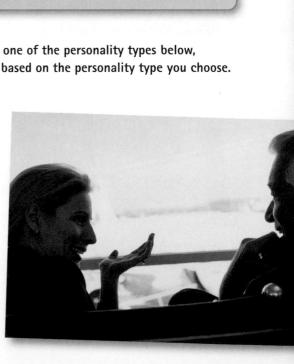

E Pair work. Follow the steps below.

1. Guess your partner's personality type.
2. Change personality types and repeat the role play.

Personality

| Lesson B | What type are you? |

1 GET READY TO READ

Describing character

What kind of personality do you have?
How about your friends? Your family?

A Pair work. There are many different ways to assess personality. Which ways below are you familiar with? What do you know about them? Discuss it with a partner.

astrology   blood type   numerology   palm reading

> **Using prefixes and suffixes**
>
> To guess the meaning of new words pay attention to prefixes, suffixes, and familiar parts of the word (e.g., *drive* in the word *driven*).

B Pair work. Study the personality adjectives in blue. Circle the word on the right that has the same or a similar meaning. Check your answers with a partner.

1. peaceful   a. nervous   b. calm
2. driven   a. ambitious   b. lazy
3. easygoing   a. strict   b. relaxed
4. assertive   a. direct   b. shy
5. unpredictable   a. expected   b. changeable

6. optimistic   a. negative   b. positive
7. nurturing   a. comforting   b. upsetting
8. systematic   a. messy   b. orderly
9. refined   a. well-mannered   b. impolite
10. introspective   a. shallow   b. thoughtful

C Pair work. Before you take the quiz on page 32, read the passage that follows. Then discuss the questions below with a partner.

1. According to this passage, where does the idea of "the five elements" come from?
2. What are the five elements and where do they exist?
3. What happens if the five elements are not in balance?

The Five Elements

Traditional Chinese medicine teaches us that there is a set of five elements, or five kinds of energy: wood, water, metal, fire, and earth. They exist everywhere and in everyone. Our feelings and personality and even our body can be described using the five elements. People who work with the five elements think it is important to keep these energies in balance in order to maintain harmony and happiness in our life. If we have too much of one element or not enough of another, trouble may occur.

A Answer questions 1–4 below. Check as many items as apply.

Spotlight on . . . Personality

1. Which word(s) describe you?

☐ assertive   ☐ easygoing   ☐ nurturing   ☐ peaceful   ☐ systematic

☐ driven   ☐ introspective   ☐ optimistic   ☐ refined   ☐ unpredictable

2. Which color(s) do you like?

☐ black   ☐ green   ☐ red   ☐ yellow   ☐ white

3. Which type(s) of food do you usually eat?

☐ bitter (leafy green vegetables)   ☐ spicy   ☐ salty   ☐ sweet

☐ sour (citrus fruits, pickled vegetables)

4. Which season(s) do you look forward to?

☐ winter   ☐ spring   ☐ summer   ☐ autumn

Score

Water _____ Wood _____ Fire _____ Earth _____ Metal _____

B Now read the description of each element on page 33. As you read, circle the words you checked in **A**. Then write the number of circled words for each element in the *Score* section.

C Read the article again. Find these facts in the reading.

According to the passage, which element is associated with . . .

1. a caring and nurturing parent? _____
2. peaceful thought and saving energy? _____
3. great energy and powerful emotions? _____
4. a time of choosing the most important things? _____
5. new beginnings and growth? _____
6. time alone? _____
7. being a risk taker? _____
8. decorating one's surroundings? _____
9. perfectionism? _____
10. spaciousness and simplicity? _____

D Pair work. Find one negative personality adjective that describes each element in the reading. What does each adjective mean? Compare your answers with a partner.

Water _____   Fire _____   Metal _____

Wood _____   Earth _____

Understanding the Five Elements

The passage below describes each element in detail, and outlines the effects each has on an individual's personality and behavior.

WATER 水

This element is represented by the color black and the calm stillness of winter. Like this season, water energy is associated with quiet reflection and the conservation and storage of energy and strength.

People whose dominant element is water have a preference for salty foods. They tend to be peaceful and introspective, though they can also be stubborn individuals who resist change. Water people value privacy and rarely share their personal thoughts and feelings with others.

Individuals with very little water often lack good sense. They tend to have a difficult time making decisions and often give up easily.

WOOD 木

This element is represented by the color green and the rebirth of spring. Wood energy is associated with youth, expansion, and the making of future plans and decisions.

People whose dominant element is wood have a preference for sour foods. They tend to be driven, assertive individuals, which can sometimes make them argumentative and difficult to get along with. Wood people are idealists who believe that there is a "right way" of doing things. However, they can also be understanding, helpful individuals who are happy to assist others in need.

Those with little or no wood tend to have a difficult time forming their own opinions and are easily persuaded by others.

FIRE 火

Not surprisingly, this element corresponds to the color red and the season of summer. Fire energy is associated with openness and abundance as well as with strong emotions such as love and joy.

People whose dominant element is fire have a preference for bitter foods. They tend to be optimistic, energetic, unpredictable individuals. Fire people often have strong opinions, and are, by nature, risk takers: they are passionate people who love excitement and change. Like fire, though, they can also be destructive and may hurt or offend others with their short tempers.

People with little or no fire tend to worry a lot and have very little self-confidence.

EARTH 土

This element is represented by the color yellow and is related to late summer—a time of wellbeing when all things are in balance.

People whose dominant element is earth have a preference for sweet foods. Earth people enjoy collecting things and decorating their surroundings. They are slow to change their minds and rarely lose their tempers. Like "Mother Earth" they project an image of comfort and stability. Earth people tend to be easygoing, caring, and nurturing, although like some parents, they can also be overprotective.

People who lack earth tend to ignore others' advice and opinions and will frequently break their promises.

METAL 金

This element is represented by the color white and is related to the season of autumn—the time when we select the essentials, and let go of waste in preparation for winter.

People whose dominant element is metal have a preference for spicy foods. They tend to be systematic and refined, but are sometimes viewed by others as somewhat distant or aloof. Metal people work best in disciplined, organized environments. They like wide, open spaces, and prefer simplicity in their surroundings. Too much clutter or decoration makes a metal person uncomfortable.

Individuals who lack metal tend to have a difficult time making quick decisions and expressing their true feelings.

▶ **Ask & Answer**

Which element(s) are dominant in your personality (i.e., have higher scores)?

Which element(s) do you have very little of (have lower scores)?

Do you agree with the description of your personality? Why or why not?

3 WRITING
Describing a location

A Pair work. Read the paragraph below. Then look around the room you're in now.
What are three things you would change? Compare your answers with a partner.

In this unit, you read that it's important to keep the five elements in balance to create harmony in your life. This theory can also be applied to many things—including decorating a home or an office. In fact, some people believe that the atmosphere of a place—the lighting, the arrangement of furniture, the color, the temperature, and the plants—can all make a big difference.

B Think of an indoor location (a café, a bedroom, a club) you like. What are the features of the place that make it feel good to be there? Include the lighting, the furniture, the colors, the smells, and so on. List the features here.

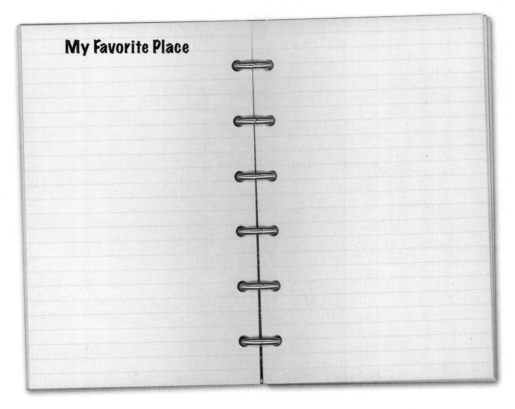

My Favorite Place

C Write a paragraph about the place in B. Begin your paragraph with a topic sentence and use the words and phrases below to organize your paragraph.

Topic sentence: There are several reasons why _____ is my favorite place.

> First of all, . . .   In addition, . . .
> Another reason is . . .   Finally, . . .

There are several reasons why The Crystal Café is my favorite place. First of all, the café has big windows, so it's always well-lit. Another reason is . . .

D Pair work. Read your partner's paragraph. Ask your partner about details that aren't clear to you. Answer the questions below.

1. What does the paragraph tell you about your partner's personality?
2. How do your favorite places compare? Are they similar or very different?

4 COMMUNICATION

Activity 1: Who do we vote off?

A Read the information below about a reality show.

A new reality TV show follows Noel Barnes and the staff of Blow Dry, a trendy hair salon in Beverly Hills, California through the first year of business. Noel Barnes opened the salon a year ago and currently employs four people. On tonight's show, Noel needs to save money and is going to have to let one of his employees go. Who should it be and why?

About her: She is a driven go-getter. Many of her clients are well-known celebrities. She often argues with Noel about how to run the salon. She gossips a lot with clients about other clients.

Name: Keiko **Job:** senior stylist

About him: He is a friend of Noel's. He is a friendly team player who gets along well with everyone. He is new and isn't bringing much money into the salon. He has a good rapport with clients and is very professional.

Name: Drew **Job:** stylist

About her: She is a hardworking self-starter who manages the day-to-day operations of the salon. Her father is a major investor in Blow Dry. She is friendly with customers, but perhaps talks too much.

Name: Yasmin **Job:** Noel's assistant

About him: He is Blow Dry's most popular stylist. Although he sometimes is rude, clients come from far away to have him cut their hair. He is a bit of a troublemaker. He has an unpredictable temper. He gives great haircuts.

Name: Jon **Job:** stylist

B Group work. Discuss the following questions. Explain your answers to the class.

1. Who should Noel let go?
2. Why that person and not one of the others?

> **Real English**
> let someone go = fire an employee

Activity 2: He's a bit of a shy person . . .

With a partner, take turns playing this game.

1. Choose one item each from Group A and B.
2. Make sentences about yourself or someone you know. Explain your answers.
3. Cross off each square in your chart as you use it.

> *My friend Pat is a bit of a shy person. For example . . .*

Group A		
a really	a complete	such
a bit	so	a bit of

Group B		
friendly salon	talkative	a pushover
a shy person	homebody	lazy

 Check out the CNN® video. **Practice your English online at elt.heinle.com/worldpass**

Unit 3: Personality

A Study the phrases in the box and think of examples from your own life.
Then use the phrases to complete the sentences below.

> **Word combinations with *personality***
>
> *a strong personality* = a person who is forceful or aggressive
> *a split personality* = a person who has two opposite characteristics
> *a personality clash* = a disagreement between people who are very different
> *a personality disorder* = a psychological illness
> *a personality trait* = a characteristic
> *a TV/radio/sports personality* = a celebrity

1. My best friend really has _____. At work, he's very aggressive, but he's a real
   pushover with his family.
2. I had to leave my job because of _____ with my boss. She was a real control
   freak who disagreed with practically everything I did.
3. Nathan's brother is _____. He played on the national soccer team, and now he's
   a well-known coach.
4. A person who has _____ is often driven and assertive.
5. _____ is a kind of disease.
6. Being lazy and messy are two _____ that I really dislike.

B Match the antonyms for personality. Then circle the ones that describe you!

1. optimistic ____
2. messy ____
3. nervous ____
4. well-mannered ____
5. stubborn ____
6. systematic ____
7. shallow ____
8. argumentative ____
9. lazy ____
10. aloof ____

a. flexible
b. driven
c. friendly
d. calm
e. organized
f. disorganized
g. rude
h. agreeable
i. introspective
j. pessimistic

Incorrect: *Would you like to join us in a cup of coffee?*   **Correct:** *Would you like to join us <u>for</u> a cup of coffee?*

Expansion Pages

C Complete the sentences with the noun that has a meaning related to the underlined adjective.

> control freak　　overachiever
> hothead　　pushover

1. My boss is totally <u>driven</u>. I'd say she's a real _____.
2. Jun-Ho is very <u>easy-going</u>. In fact, he's a total _____.
3. My brother is very <u>unpredictable</u> and gets angry easily. He's a real _____.
4. Dr. Sanchez is a little bit too <u>systematic</u>. Frankly, I'd have to say he's a real _____.

D Circle one word in each set that doesn't fit. Use your dictionary as necessary.

1. peaceful	easygoing	calm	driven
2. harmony	conflict	peace	stillness
3. extrovert	privacy	introspective	personal
4. salty	loud	sour	bitter
5. aloof	assertive	aggressive	argumentative
6. optimistic	joyful	gloomy	cheerful
7. risk-taker	cautious	unpredictable	passionate
8. contentment	well-being	disappointment	satisfaction

E Read the first sentence and pay attention to the word in bold.
Then circle the word in parentheses that best completes its meaning.

1. In my opinion, Jack is completely **unreliable**. You (can / shouldn't) rely on him for anything.
2. My parents were **overprotective** when I was a child. They (seldom / always) let me try risky things.
3. Dale is a very **thoughtful** person. He thinks (a lot / very little) about other people.
4. I had a very **uncaring** teacher last year. She really (was / wasn't) concerned about her students' success.
5. Government employees need to be more **cooperative**. They need to work (alone / together) for the good of the country.
6. Don't be so **careless**! You really have to (pay more attention / stop worrying).

In Other Words

An **ambitious** person has a strong desire to be successful: *Vera is really ambitious about becoming a physicist and winning the Nobel Prize!*
If someone is **motivated**, he or she has strong reasons for doing something: *Jun-Ho is motivated to improve his English because he's moving to Canada next month.*
Determined means not letting anyone stop you: *The team was determined to win the championship game.*
Pushy (informal) refers to someone who is unpleasantly aggressive in getting what they want: *That car salesman was really pushy about trying to sell me an SUV.*

Describe means to tell what something is like: *She described her hometown / the ceremony / his personality.*
Explain means to make something clear and easy to understand: *He explained the reasons / the situation / how to use the machine.*
Portray means to describe according to one's own view: *The movie portrayed doctors as greedy and uncaring.*

 **Watch out!**

relationship adverbs
Use only one adverb in each sentence to show the relationship between clauses.
> She's my best friend, <u>so</u> I understand her problems.
> <u>Because</u> she's my best friend, I understand her problems.
> ~~<u>Because</u> she's my best friend, <u>so</u> I understand her problems.~~

Review: Units 1–3

1 LANGUAGE CHECK

There is a mistake in the underlined part of each sentence. Rewrite each underlined section correctly. One sentence has no mistakes. Write OK next to it.

1. All tourists entering our country <u>has to be checked</u> for the proper visa. _____ have to be checked _____
2. Do you know whether the computer <u>has repaired yet</u>? _____
3. I like to go to bed early <u>although I'll</u> feel well rested the next day. _____
4. I traveled in Southeast Asia last year, but <u>I've never went</u> to China. _____
5. My parents and <u>I lived in the same house</u> since 1989. _____
6. I think Mi-Ran <u>has graduated from</u> Seoul National University two years ago. _____
7. Hybrid cars <u>can be buy</u> in a limited number of countries so far. _____
8. <u>Though my job interview</u> is tomorrow at 8 A.M., I think I should catch the bus at 7:15. _____
9. <u>Rita has goes</u> on a diet every year on January 1, but she never loses any weight. _____
10. What has been the most interesting topic <u>that we were studied</u>? _____
11. Whenever we <u>go for vacation</u>, we like to plan everything in advance. _____
12. People <u>are sometimes surprising</u> to learn that TV was invented in 1927. _____
13. In 1999, <u>I've quit my job</u> in London and moved to Brussels. _____
14. <u>Even though I forget</u> her birthday every year, my girlfriend still loves me. _____
15. Radioactivity <u>was discovered from</u> Marie Curie in the nineteenth century. _____

2 VOCABULARY CHECK

Read the article and use the word in parentheses to form a new word or phrase to complete the sentence.

I read a really interesting article by a woman named Brenda Gaines—it's the (**1**. cover) _____ cover story _____ in *Business 2000* magazine this week. She's a reporter for the magazine, and to (**2**. piece) _____ a story explaining the poor customer service at a cell phone company, she secretly got a job as a representative and worked there for a month.

Ms. Gaines said it almost ruined her life. For one thing, she had to start work at 6 A.M., and she's never been (**3**. rise) _____. All day, she was completely overloaded with work. She had only two minutes to deal with each phone call, even if the customer had a complicated problem. She said that didn't give her enough time for (**4**. act) _____ with the callers. The job involved constant (**5**. task) _____—she had to answer her phone, fill out forms, and respond to e-mail, often all at the same time.

When she first started the assignment, she says she was a real (**6**. get) _____, and truly wanted to help the customers. But some of them were terrible (**7**. hot) _____ who shouted and even cursed at her. And her supervisor sounded like a complete (**8**. control) _____—he even recorded how much time each employee spent in the bathroom! Gaines was finally fired from her job after a month because they said she wasn't a (**9**. play) _____ and didn't work well with her colleagues.

Gaines's story is easy to believe—you can't (**10**. make) _____ details like that. And she made an important point. Cell phone companies need to end their (**11**. heavy) _____ on undertrained, badly paid workers. There is too much (**12**. at) _____. If customers receive poor service, they will take their business elsewhere.

3 NOW YOU'RE TALKING!

Situation 3

A Pair work. Choose one of the pictures and imagine yourselves in the situation. What would the people talk about? Briefly review the language notes from Units 1–3.

B Pair work. Read the statements in C and add two of your own goals. Then role-play the situation you chose keeping your speaking goals in mind.

C Now rate your speaking. Use + for good, ✓ for OK, and – for things you need to improve.

How did you do?	
I spoke loudly enough for my partner(s) to hear me.	
I spoke without too much hesitation.	
I spoke at a good rate of speed—not too fast or too slow.	
I used new vocabulary from the units.	
I used at least three expressions from the units.	
I practiced the grammar from the units.	
My own goals: 1. _____ 2. _____	

Make an Impact

Lesson A | Change your world

1 VOCABULARY FOCUS
Generational differences

What three words would you use to describe your friends
and others of your generation? An older generation?

A Pair work. These words and phrases are used in the reading below. Circle the ones that are familiar
to you. Look at the roots of the unfamiliar words. With a partner, can you guess their meanings?

visionary	escapist	activist	motivated	circumstances
be aware of	generation	issues	tradition	apathetic

B Read each opinion and complete the statement that follows.

Gary

Where are all the young visionaries—the people who want to make a difference
in the world? It seems that most of the younger generation are so escapist:
they're too busy watching TV, playing video games, and making money to
care about the issues facing the world. Instead of "slacking off," they could
be making a difference. Back in the sixties and seventies we were activists:
we marched and protested to change our world. Who is going to carry on this
tradition of activism?

He thinks _____.

Briana

The people of my generation are not slackers! Many of us are motivated and
care about what's happening in the world—we're not as apathetic as you make
us sound. We're very aware of the problems in the world today and know that
we have a role to play in creating a positive future. But our circumstances are
different from yours, so don't expect us to do things the same way.

She thinks _____.

C Circle the correct answers.

1. A **visionary** has positive ideas about the past / future.
2. People in the same **generation** are roughly the
   same age / personality type.
3. An **escapist** thinks a lot about real / imaginary life.
4. An **issue** is an important problem or subject /
   conversation that people are discussing.
5. An **activist** works for / avoids social or political change.
6. To **carry on a tradition** means to stop / continue
   doing something from the past.

7. A **motivated** person is determined / unsure about
   something.
8. An **apathetic** person is uninterested in / curious
   about everything.
9. To **be aware of** something is to know / guess that
   something exists or is happening.
10. The **circumstances** of your life are the overall
    factors / people that influence your life.

▷▷ Vocabulary Builder ▲

The prefix *a* in the word *apathetic* means "not" or "without."
Read each sentence below and paraphrase it.

1. Julio was <u>apolitical</u>. <u>Julio wasn't interested in politics</u> .
2. Cats are <u>asocial</u> animals. _____
3. These days, it's <u>atypical</u> to have more than two children.
   _____
4. He's a completely <u>amoral</u> person.
   _____

2 LISTENING
A summer internship

If you could do an internship, what kind of organization would you like to work for? What would you like to learn about as an intern?

Real English
An *internship* is a short-term, supervised work experience related to a student's major program and/or career plans.

A **Read this ad about an internship opportunity. Then listen and answer the questions.** (CD Tracks 10 & 11)

1. Where do you think this conversation is taking place?
   _____
2. Who is Samir? _____
3. Who is Jeff? _____
4. Who is Marcie? _____

Intern for the summer at the Foundation for Global Issues (FGI) Wanted: Intelligent, outgoing individual to work in our office. Must be self-motivated and have good writing/speaking/listening skills. Computer friendly and good with numbers helpful. Unique opportunity to learn about global activism.

B **Listen again. What will Samir be doing? Complete the list.** (CD Track 12)

1. attending <u>meetings with government officials and their staff</u>
2. taking _____
3. writing _____
4. analyzing _____
5. updating _____

C **Pair work. Look back at the ad in A. How do the qualities that FGI is looking for relate to Samir's job responsibilities?**

FGI is looking for someone with good writing skills. Samir will be taking notes during important meetings.

▶ **Ask & Answer**
Does Samir's internship sound interesting to you? Do you think it's a job you could do? Why or why not?

D **Based on what you know about Samir's internship, which tasks do you think he might work on in the future? Check (✓) the boxes.**

☐ measuring the difference in world population between five years ago and today
☐ hiring new staff for the office

☐ creating a new web site for FGI
☐ leading a meeting with government officials
☐ writing the announcement of a new FGI program

A Pair work. Read what Ana wrote about her family's effort to conserve water. Circle the best answer for each item. Check answers with a partner.

Last summer, it hardly rained. During that time, water use was restricted and we (1. weren't allowed to / weren't required to) water our lawns during the day. My family (2. should have / may have) followed that law, but we didn't and we (3. were able to / had to) pay a fine to the city. Our family (4. has to / had to) change our regular routines after that. We became more aware of the whole issue of water use, and ways to cut back. First, you (5. should / shouldn't) leave the water running when brushing your teeth. It doesn't seem like a lot of water, but every drop adds up. Second, although we all (6. have to / don't have to) drink a lot of water every day to stay healthy, we (7. should / shouldn't) buy bottled water because sometimes we just want a sip or two, and the rest goes into the trash. Third, reuse the towels when you stay in a hotel more than one night. You (8. have to / don't have to) have a clean towel every day. I became aware that each one of us (9. can / should) make a difference with a little effort. By the end of the summer, our family (10. is permitted to / was permitted to) water our lawn again. We're still motivated to keep up our new habits, though.

B Complete the chart below with an appropriate modal or modal phrase. Use the information in A to help you.

Present	Past
ability ___ *am/is/are able to*	ability *could* *was/were able to*
giving permission *can/may* *am/is/are permitted to* ___ / ___ / ___ _____ ___	giving permission *could* ___ / ___ _____ ___ *was/were allowed to*
necessity *must* _____ ___ *am/is/are required to*	necessity *had to* *was/were required to*
lack of necessity *don't/doesn't have to*	lack of necessity _____ _____ _____
advice _____ *shouldn't*	advice/regret *should have* *shouldn't have*

C Pair work. Use the chart in B to complete the conversations below. Use the affirmative or negative form. More than one answer may be possible. Compare your answers with a partner.

1. A: I'm graduating next year and don't know what to do next.
   B: In my opinion, you _____ go to college. Otherwise, how will you get a good job?

2. A: How was the exhibit at the art museum?
   B: Great! Best of all, it was free! I _____ pay a thing.

3. A: Who did you support in the last election?
   B: I _____ vote then. I was too young at the time.

4. A: It's impossible to change anything in the world.
   B: That's not true. You _____ make a difference. You just _____ get involved first.

5. A: He _____ complete his job application by Monday, but he didn't.
   B: He's so apathetic. He doesn't seem to care about anything.

6. A: Why _____ we hire you for this internship?
   B: Well, for one thing I _____ talk about the issues. I'm very well informed.

7. A: _____ I call you to discuss this tomorrow?
   B: I'm sorry, but I _____ do it tomorrow. How about Friday?

8. A: How's work going? Did you _____ work overtime to make your deadline last week?
   B: Yeah, I did. But, I _____ go to work on Thursday or Friday this week, so I'm happy.

CLASSIFIED JOBS March 18

ACTIVITIES COORDINATOR

D Group work. Read about this job opportunity aboard the Peace Boat. Then follow the steps below.

We are currently accepting applications for Activities Coordinator on the Peace Boat, an international non-profit organization that travels throughout the world from Japan on "peace voyages." Participants visit different countries and meet local people to promote peace, human rights, and respect for the environment.

The Coordinator can join Peace Boat participants in all activities on shore. The Coordinator will interview with us, but it is not necessary to come to Tokyo to do so. All expenses will be covered for the trip, but the Coordinator is responsible for obtaining a passport and proper immunizations. Without these, the Coordinator cannot board the ship.

Job requirements: speak some English; ability to prepare students on board for cultural exchange activities with locals (such as soccer games, mural painting, and tree planting). Preferred but not necessary: speak some Spanish and Japanese; experience in teaching sports and art.

1. Discuss the job requirements for the Activities Coordinator by completing these sentences:

a. The candidate has to . . .   c. He or she absolutely must . . .   e. It's OK if the Coordinator can't . . .
b. He or she is required to . . .   d. He or she doesn't have to . . .   f. The Coordinator is permitted to . . .

2. Do you think you'd be right for the job? Why or why not? Tell your group.

4 SPEAKING

I hate to disagree with you, but . . .

A Pair work. Read the two conversations. What is the relationship between the speakers in each one?

Conversation 1

Ginny:	I really think we need to cut out the kids' computer classes. Between that and soccer practice, they have no free time at all after school.
Doug:	I'm not so sure about that. They're in middle school now, and they need to know about computers.
Ginny:	Oh, come on! They were still doing homework at 10:00 last night.
Doug:	Really? Well, you may be right about the lessons, then. Kids need time to just play.

Conversation 2

Mr. Yuan:	The way I see it, what we need is an advertising campaign that will shock people.
Ms. Perez:	That seems a little bit extreme. I think it's better to give the facts about our products.
Mr. Yuan:	I hate to disagree with you, but people don't remember facts—they remember images.
Ms. Perez:	You may be right in part, but there's so much shock advertising these days. We need to try something unique—like using humor to give information.
Mr. Yuan:	You may have something there. What would you suggest?

B Fill in the chart with these expressions. Then add the expressions in blue from the conversations on page 43.

> I see your point, but . . .
> Exactly!
> Definitely!
>
> I completely agree.
> No way!
> I'm not sure I agree with you.
>
> You're absolutely right!
> I know what you mean, but . . .
> Yeah, but . . . I don't think so.

Agreeing with an opinion	Disagreeing with an opinion

C Pair work. Answer the questions.

1. Which expressions would you use when talking to a friend or coworker?
2. Which expressions would you be more likely to use with someone you didn't know as well?
3. What are some things that you disagree with your friends/family/coworkers about?
   Do you ever try to change their opinions?

D Pair work. Choose role A or B, and think about reasons for your opinions.
Then role-play these situations with your partner.

1. A: After finishing high school, you want to start your own business instead of going to university.
   B: You're A's friend. You think this is a terrible idea.

2. A: You want to set up a recycling program in your office.
   B: You're A's boss. You think this would be impractical.

3. A: You belong to Stop Hunger Now. You want to have a benefit concert to raise money.
   B: You're also a member. You think it's better just to ask people to donate money.

4. A: You're planning a class party. You want to have it in a restaurant so that people can get to know each other.
   B: You're A's classmate. You think a party at a dance club would be more fun.

Make an Impact

Lesson B | Take a stand.

1 GET READY TO READ

Take action!

 What ads have made an impression on you? Why?

A Pair work. Read each ad and discuss the questions below.

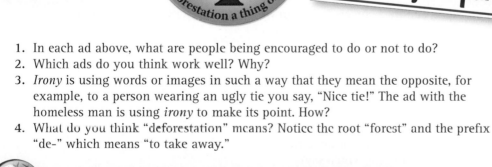

1. In each ad above, what are people being encouraged to do or not to do?
2. Which ads do you think work well? Why?
3. *Irony* is using words or images in such a way that they mean the opposite, for example, to a person wearing an ugly tie you say, "Nice tie!" The ad with the homeless man is using *irony* to make its point. How?
4. What do you think "deforestation" means? Notice the root "forest" and the prefix "de-" which means "to take away."

World Link

Experts say that the biggest single step to curbing global warming is raising vehicular gas mileage standards. By requiring SUVs and other light trucks to get the same gas mileage as cars, 240 million tons of carbon dioxide per year would be saved by the end of the next decade.

▶ **Ask & Answer**
Have you ever seen an ad, poster, bumper sticker, or button like the ones above? What did it say? What was it encouraging people to do or not to do?

A Pair work. The reading on page 47 is about a company that promotes the events below. What kind of company do you think it is? What do you think they want to have happen for each of these events? Discuss your ideas with your partner.

Buy Nothing Day   No Car Day   TV Turnoff Week

B Read the article on page 47. Then read the statements in the chart. Were these ideas stated in the article, or did you have to infer this information? Check the correct box. Then compare your answers with a partner.

	stated	inferred
1. Kalle Lasn made documentaries for public television in Canada for years.		
2. Kalle Lasn and his partners believe that advertising should be used to inform people, not just sell them products.		
3. The Culture Jammers Network is made up of people who are interested in social change.		
4. Lasn believes that people shouldn't just complain. They need to try to change things they're unhappy about.		
5. It's now possible to see some of Adbusters ads on cable TV stations.		

C Read the article again. Pay attention to details about ways Kalle Lasn thinks outside the box. Then complete the sentences below with information from the reading.

1. Unlike other advertisements, many of Adbuster's ads use _____ and _____ to promote a _____ message.
2. Culture Jammers hosts events such as _____, _____, and _____.
   The goal with these events is to _____.
3. To challenge how people think, some Culture Jammers hack into web sites in order to
   _____.
4. Lasn's motto is _____.

Real English
think outside the box = think differently or in an original and creative way

D Pair work. Discuss the questions below.

1. What is the main point of the ad for "Hope" cigarettes?
2. If the mother of the baby in the fast-food ad could speak to the president of the company, what do you think she would say?

▶ **Ask & Answer**
Adbusters sponsors events like TV Turnoff Week. Think about your daily routine. What's one change you could make that would make a difference?

ADBUSTERS

THINK OUTSIDE THE BOX

Kalle Lasn was in a supermarket parking lot one afternoon when he had an experience that changed his life. In order to shop at the store, he needed to put money into the shopping cart to use it. Annoyed that he had to "pay to shop," Lasn jammed the coin into the cart so that it wouldn't work. It was an act of rebellion—the first of many—for Lasn.

Born in Estonia, Kalle Lasn moved to Australia as a young man and then later to Japan, where he founded a marketing research firm in Tokyo. Eventually, Lasn emigrated to Canada and for several years produced documentaries for public television. In the late 1980s, Lasn made an advertisement that spoke out against the logging industry and the deforestation going on in the Pacific Northwest. When he tried to show his ad on TV, though, no station in the region would give him airtime. In response, Lasn and a colleague founded Adbusters Media Foundation, a company dedicated to the "human right to communicate."

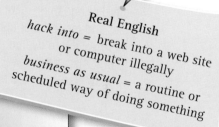

Be a considerate consumer. Don't buy fur.

Adbusters produces magazine, newspaper, and TV ads with a social message. Many use humor and irony to make their points: in one, for example, a man chain smokes a brand of cigarettes called "Hope." In another, a child is dressed in an outfit used in fast-food ads. Next to the child is a note from its mother telling the restaurant to leave her child alone.

Adbusters also has a magazine and a web site, The Culture Jammers Network, whose members include students, artists, and activists as well as educators and businesspeople interested in social change. Many of these "culture jammers" are working to raise awareness about different social issues by hosting events like "Buy Nothing Day," "No Car Day," and "TV Turnoff Week." Lasn and his partners hope these events will encourage people to think about questions such as:

- What kinds of things are we being encouraged to buy by the media?

- Should cars be our primary means of transportation?

- How are television and radio being used now? How *could* we be using them?

> **Real English**
> hack into = break into a web site or computer illegally
> business as usual = a routine or scheduled way of doing something

Some culture jammers are using other methods to challenge how people think. Some pretend to be shoppers. They move items in stores from one shelf to another making it difficult for people to find things easily. Other culture jammers hack into large corporate web sites and jam them so that they become unusable. The goal in both cases is to prevent "business as usual" and to get people to ask themselves questions such as "Why am I shopping here?" or "Why should I buy this product?"

Lasn and members of The Culture Jammers Network want to make people aware of social issues, but they also believe it's important to think of solutions, too. "[A lot of people] tell you everything that's wrong . . . but they never say much about how to fix these problems," says Lasn. [But] "there is plenty we can do. If you start despairing, you have lost everything."

Though many TV stations still won't show Adbusters' "uncommercials," some cable TV stations have started to. People all over the world have also joined the Culture Jammers Network and are doing their part to promote social change. Behind it all is Lasn's motto, "We can and must change the world."

A Read this letter to the editor of a newspaper.

NO CAR DAY
Find new ways to get there!

TV TURNOFF WEEK
Quit watching, start living!

Buy Nothing Day
Stop shopping and save the planet!

April 12

Dear Editor:

Your article about Kalle Lasn and Adbusters had some interesting ideas, especially about transportation. <u>No Car Day is a great idea for our city.</u> For one thing, a lot of drivers will learn how fast and modern our subway is. They might be more willing to use public transportation in the future. Also, people will get healthy exercise if they walk or bike. I started biking to work last year, and it has made a huge difference in my energy level. And finally, a day without cars shows how much pollution they pour into the air. Wouldn't it be great to breathe clean air, even for just one day? I think we would be shocked by the difference. No Car Day is an idea whose time has come, and I hope the city council will support it.

Sincerely,
Natalia Moreno

B Reread the underlined sentence where Natalia gives her opinion.
This is the *topic sentence.* Then write the three ideas she includes to support her opinion.

1. _____
2. _____
3. _____

C Complete this topic sentence for your own letter to the editor. Then list three reasons for your opinion.

In my opinion, (TV Turnoff Week / Buy Nothing Day) is a (great / terrible) idea.

Reasons:
1. _____
2. _____
3. _____

D Write your own letter to the editor.

E Pair work. Exchange letters with a partner. Make two suggestions to help your partner improve his or her letter. If you don't like your partner's suggestions, disagree politely.

I think you need to explain your reasons a little more.

I see your point, but letters to the editor have to be short.

Activity 1: What's your motto?

A Kalle Lasn's motto is "We can and must change the world." What's your personal motto? Choose one from the ones here or write your own.

Through it all, keep smiling.

Die trying.

Be prepared.

EVERYONE DESERVES A SECOND CHANCE.

Accept what you can't change and change what you can't accept.

To thine own self be true.

Your idea: _____

Waste not, want not.

B Group work. Get into a group of three or four people. Tell your group what your motto is. Describe a situation in which your motto has helped you.

Activity 2: A public service announcement

A Pair work. Listen to the Public Service Announcement. Then discuss the questions with a partner. (CD Tracks 13 & 14)

1. What issue is the PSA trying to raise awareness about?
2. What is it telling people they should or shouldn't do?

Real English
Public Service Announcements (PSAs) are short radio or TV ads used to raise public awareness about an issue.

B Group work. Work in groups of three to write a short PSA to raise awareness about a specific issue. Choose an issue from below or think of your own.

- eating right
- driving safely
- recycling
- saving money
- promoting peace
- other: _____

C Class work. Present your PSA to the class. As you listen to your classmates' PSAs, answer questions 1 and 2 in A for each.

CNN. ® Check out the CNN® video. Practice your English online at <u>elt.thomson.com/worldpass</u>

Unit 4: Make an Impact

A Match each word in blue with its meaning.

1. Animal rights **activists** have been campaigning for all of us to stop eating meat. ___
2. Surfing and scuba diving are two of my favorite vacation **activities**. ___
3. There has been an increase in **activism** among students in recent years. ___
4. My grandmother stays **active** with gardening, playing cards, and going to her senior citizens' club. ___
5. People should be **proactive** and prepare for natural disasters. ___
6. Ms. Jemison will be the **acting** manager until we hire someone permanently. ___

a. working for social change (noun)
b. things that people do for a purpose or for relaxation (noun)
c. busy doing things (adjective)
d. taking charge of things before they happen (adjective)
e. temporary (adjective)
f. people who work for social change (noun)

B Complete the sentences with a form of a word from **A**. Add an article (*a, an, the*) where necessary.

1. When I was younger, I led a very _____ life. I played on two sports teams, and I went hiking in the mountains almost every weekend.
2. Skydiving is _____ that I've never tried. It's just too dangerous.
3. It's better to take a _____ approach to pollution than to spend money on it later.
4. My best friend is _____ for an environmental group called "Save the Oceans."
5. The new _____ principal of the school held a meeting to introduce herself to the teachers.
6. "Adbusters" is an example of _____ against overconsumption.

> **I didn't know that!**
>
> *Candidate* comes from the Latin word *candidus*, which means "bright, shining white." In ancient Rome, candidates who hoped to be elected to government office would wear bright white clothes. The English word *candid*, which means "honest," comes from the same source. But how many *candidates* are really *candid*?

C Fill in the blanks with the related strong adjective in the box.

boiling	gorgeous	terrifying	enormous	freezing	tiny	horrendous

1. The weather was <u>cold</u> yesterday, and it's even colder today. In fact, it's _____.
2. My dog is <u>small</u>, but my sister's dog is absolutely _____.
3. Our classroom is usually too <u>warm</u>, but today it's _____ in here.
4. That movie isn't just <u>scary</u>. I think it's _____!
5. Her old house was <u>big</u>, but her new house is really _____.
6. The storm wasn't just <u>bad</u>. It was truly _____.
7. Carmen isn't just <u>beautiful</u>. I think she's absolutely _____.

D Rewrite the sentences using one of the phrases from the box.

Word combinations with *action*	
no further action is needed	swing into action
plan of action	call for action
take action	put your ideas into action

1. The city government must <u>do something</u> to solve the transportation crisis.

   _____

2. Firefighters are always ready to <u>start working immediately</u> in case of any emergency.

   _____

3. We have received your application, and at this time, <u>you don't need to do anything else</u>.

   _____

4. You have a great plan, and now it's time to <u>start doing something about your idea</u>.

   _____

5. "Save the Earth" has issued a <u>request for help</u> to stop the construction of a giant hotel on Paradise Beach.

   _____

6. We need to develop a <u>list of future activities</u> for our campaign to improve education in this country.

   _____

E Review these words from the reading "Think Outside the Box" on page 47. Circle their meanings.

1. rebellion (para 1)   a. getting ready   b. making noise   c. fighting back
2. logging (para 2)   a. cutting trees   b. building houses   c. killing animals
3. primary (para 4)   a. most expensive   b. most important   c. most unusual
4. despairing (para 6)   a. giving up   b. making plans   c. being hopeful
5. promote (para 7)   a. stop   b. protest   c. increase

In Other Words

If you are **apathetic**, you are not willing to make an effort to change things: *My parents are completely apathetic about environmental problems.*

If you are **indifferent** to something, you have no feelings about it: *Alan was crazy about Cathy, but she was indifferent to him.*

Uninterested means not interested: *I'm completely uninterested in baseball. I think it's boring.*

Disinterested is NOT the same as uninterested. It means "not influenced by personal reasons": *We need a disinterested person to decide what is fair.*

An **obligation** is a legal or moral requirement: *Teachers have an obligation to treat all their students fairly.*

A **responsibility** means the state of being in charge of something: *Janet will have responsibility for the new advertising campaign.*

Duties (usually plural) are parts of a job: *My duties include feeding and taking care of the zoo animals.*

A **requirement** is something that is essential or needed: *The requirements for that job are a master's degree and five years' experience.*

 **Watch out!**

negative prefixes

The prefixes *a-, un-, in-/il-/im-* used with adjectives all have the meaning "not" or "without." However, you have to learn which prefix goes with which adjective.

perfect	→ *imperfect*	~~unperfect, aperfect~~
political	→ *apolitical*	~~unpolitical, impolitical~~
motivated	→ *unmotivated*	~~amotivated, immotivated~~

Believe It or Not

Lesson A | Mysterious disappearances

1 VOCABULARY FOCUS

A mysterious disappearance

 You are going to read a news article based on a police report. What kinds of news events are typically in a police report?

A Read the article. What kind of police report is it based on? Check (✓) the box.

☐ burglary report   ☐ traffic report   ☐ missing persons report

---

Daily Times   Tuesday, September 22

Somerville Man Sought

A Somerville man, is being **sought** by police after he disappeared on Friday afternoon. Adam Martin, a well-known family man and **devoted** father of two, left home September 19th and never returned.

Police say that Martin, 39, went out at 2:00 P.M. with his tool kit, saying he was answering a **distress call** from his friend Devin, who was **stranded** on the Highway 92 with a flat tire. By late Friday evening, his wife Susan was very worried. She considered calling the police, but decided to wait until the following morning to contact **authorities**.

Martin, a banker, had the day off, because his branch of First Bank Savings & Loan was closed for renovations. "He seemed very relaxed and happy to have some time away from the office," said his wife. "I didn't notice anything out of the ordinary."

Police are eager to question Martin about a bank transfer he made late Thursday night. "A large amount of cash was transferred from our branch in Somerville to the main branch in Boston late Thursday night," said First Bank

manager Frank de Leo. "The money was then withdrawn in Boston on Friday afternoon."

Police are speaking with a **witness** who may have seen Martin on Friday afternoon in a bright blue truck with an unidentified young female passenger. The female is also being sought for questioning regarding her **involvement** in the case.

Mrs. Martin is keeping her hopes up. "Adam has **seemingly vanished**—which is completely unlike him," says Susan. "But I know that this story will have a positive **outcome**. I know that he will return soon."

A blue truck was found on Monday about a half mile from the airport. It has been **identified** as Mr. Martin's. Inside the truck were some bank **documents** and a pair of sunglasses. Police are studying this **evidence** carefully.

Police may have a **theory** about what happened, but are not talking at the moment. They urge anyone with information regarding this **incident** to call the Somerville Police at 800-555-TIPS.

B Write the words in A next to their definitions below.

1. a person who sees an event: __witness__
2. official papers: _____
3. looked for: _____
4. apparently: _____
5. an emergency call for help: _____
6. recognized: _____
7. officials, in this case the police: _____
8. disappeared suddenly: _____

9. words or objects that prove something is true: _____
10. in a helpless situation and unable to move: _____
11. event: _____
12. result: _____
13. dedicated: _____
14. participation: _____
15. an explanation not yet proven to be true: _____

C Pair work. What do you think happened to Adam Martin?
Discuss with a partner.

≫ Vocabulary Builder ▲

Some nouns are usually found in the plural. Read an update on the situation.
Use the plural nouns in the box to complete the information.

> authorities   premises   outskirts   whereabouts

(1) _____ are still searching for a missing Somerville man who disappeared last Friday. Although they don't know Adam Martin's exact (2) _____, they think he may now be in California. Yesterday they inspected a room at the Golden Gable Hotel, located on the (3) _____ of Boston. It is believed Martin stayed there on the night of Friday, September 19. When police searched the (4) _____, they found a receipt for two airline tickets to Los Angeles.

2 LISTENING
A chance meeting

> Think about a time you ran into someone. Who was it?
> Where were you? How did you feel?

A Pair work. Look at this photo. What do you think the situation is? Discuss your ideas with a partner.

B Listen. What is the relationship between Claudia and Cara? Check (✓) the box. (CD Tracks 15 & 16)

☐ They are former classmates being reunited.

☐ They are sisters who were adopted at birth by different parents.

☐ They are college friends who survived a train crash five years ago.

Real English
run into = to see someone by chance
adopt = to legally make someone else's child part of your family

C Listen to Claudia and Cara talk about their lives. Read each item.
If it's the same for the girls, write "S." If it's different, write "D." (CD Track 17)

1. _D_ religious background
2. ___ where they grew up
3. ___ their physical appearance
4. ___ college
5. ___ where they live now
6. ___ relationship with Josh now
7. ___ favorite food

Real English
We use *to say the least* to express that a statement is even more surprising or serious than has been suggested. *My father was ungry, to say the least.*

D The phrases below are used in the interview. Listen and circle to complete each answer. (CD Track 18)

1. An only child has no / many brothers and sisters.
2. When you can't tell two people apart, it's because they look the same / different.
3. A twist of fate is an expected / unexpected event.
4. If two people have a lot in common they have similar / different characteristics and habits.

E Pair work. Compare your answers in C with a partner. Then, use the phrases in D and your own words to retell Claudia's and Cara's story.

▶ **Ask & Answer**
Is adoption common in your country? Why or why not?

Modals of speculation about the past

A Read about the disappearance of Jim Thompson.

Jim Thompson was a young American when he arrived in Thailand in 1945, two days after the end of World War II. For the next 22 years, he lived in Thailand, working to revitalize the Thai silk industry, which had all but disappeared. As the founder of his own silk company, he also promoted Thai arts and crafts. Today you can tour the Jim Thompson House in Bangkok, one of the finest examples of traditional Thai architecture in the city.

In March of 1967, while vacationing in Malaysia's Cameron Highlands, Jim Thompson went for a walk. He never returned. There was no distress call, and no witnesses ever came forward with information about his disappearance or his whereabouts. The question is: What happened to Jim Thompson?

B Pair work. Look back at the modal phrases in blue below. Which theories about Jim Thompson are more certain? Underline them. Which are less certain? Circle them. Then compare your ideas with a partner.

There are many theories surrounding Jim Thompson's disappearance:

1. During the war Jim Thompson was trained by the OSS, which later became the CIA (Central Intelligency Agency) in the United States. <u>He may have worked for the CIA after the war ended.</u> If that is true, he **might have been killed** because of his connection to the CIA.

2. Some people say that he **could have decided** to start a new life somewhere else, so he disappeared on purpose. Others point to the fact that he left his cigarettes and lighter behind when he went on the walk. He **must have planned** to return, they say.

3. It's been well over 35 years since he disappeared. Most people agree that he **couldn't have survived**.

C Read more statements about Jim Thompson. Choose the appropriate response for each.

1. Jim Thompson lived in Thailand for 22 years.
   a. He may have loved the country and its people.
   b. He must have loved the country and its people.

2. Six months after Jim's disappearance, his sister was murdered by a burglar in Chicago.
   a. That's surprising. There may have been a connection.
   b. That's surprising. There must not have been any connection.

3. He could have fallen into a cave and died.
   a. I agree. I'm sure that happened.
   b. Anything is possible, I guess.

4. I don't know anything about Jim Thompson.
   a. You must not have read the book about him.
   b. You must have read the book about him.

5. He couldn't have disappeared on purpose.
   a. We can conclude that he didn't disappear on purpose.
   b. We can't conclude that he disappeared on purpose.

D Pair work. Read the conversations about Jim Thompson. Rewrite the underlined sentences using modals of speculation. Compare your answers with a partner. Then discuss what you think happened to him.

1. A: <u>Maybe he was kidnapped</u>.

   _____

   B: <u>It's certain that didn't happen</u>. There was no ransom note.

   _____

   A: <u>It's likely he had a heart attack</u>.

   _____

   B: <u>That's possible</u>.

   _____

2. A: <u>We can conclude he died in the jungle</u>.

   _____

   B: <u>It's possible he didn't die there</u>. After all, none of his clothing or bones were ever found or identified.

   _____

E Pair work. Read the situations below. Discuss them with a partner.

1. You went into your office last Sunday to pick up some documents. You surprised your coworker, who was at his desk. He seemed nervous. What do you think he was doing?

2. You arrived home late one night and saw someone climbing into your neighbor's kitchen window. Who do you think it was?

3. You were on a date when your dinner partner's cell phone rang. He/She looked upset and left the table to take the call. Who do you think was on the other end of the phone line?

F Group work. Join another pair and exchange ideas. Then vote on the most probable explanation for each situation.

The expression "raining cats and dogs" is used to mean "raining heavily." However, fish, frogs, snakes, and even apples have actually fallen from the sky! Where do these "strange rains" come from? Scientists think strong winds pick up the items and carry them a short distance before dropping them on the heads of very surprised onlookers.

4 SPEAKING
The boss's birthday cake

A **Read the situation below. Then look at the expressions in blue and match the sentence parts.**

The office workers at Zigert Co. planned to have a birthday party for their boss at lunch time today. Yesterday at 5 P.M., they put Mr. Ramero's birthday cake in the office refrigerator. When they opened the fridge this morning at 8 A.M., it was empty. What happened?

> **Making speculations**
>
> **Less certain**
> 1. I wonder if the cleaners __g__
> 2. I suppose a thief ____
> 3. I suspect that our boss ____
> 4. I'm pretty sure that Jason ____
> 5. I'm convinced/certain/positive that Mary ____
> 6. It's impossible that we ____
> 7. There's no doubt that the cake ____
> **More certain**

a. stole the cake. He loves desserts.
b. took it home with him yesterday. It had his name on it.
c. forgot to order it. We know that Carol picked it up.
d. could have broken into the office last night.
e. ate it. She was in the office until 10:00 last night.
f. was gone when we got to work.
g. ~~emptied out the fridge~~.

B **List five possible explanations for each of these situations.**

Your class started fifteen minutes ago. Your teacher still isn't there.

1. _stuck in a traffic jam_
2. _____
3. _____
4. _____
5. _____

You are at the train station to meet your friend after work. Your friend has never been there before. You have been waiting for an hour.

1. _gotten lost_
2. _____
3. _____
4. _____
5. _____

C **Pair work. Talk about the situations in B, and respond to your partner's explanations.**

> I wonder if Mr. Erikson is stuck in a traffic jam.

> No way! He walks to school.

> **Responding to speculation**
>
> Definitely!
> You're probably right.
> You may be right.
> Well, maybe, but . . .
> That hardly seems likely.
> No way! *(informal)*

D **Pair work. Think of a mysterious situation and write it down. Give it to another pair.**

> You come to class late. When you open the door, no one is there, but there's a big empty box on the teacher's desk.

E **Pair work. Role-play explaining the situation you received.**

> Somebody must have . . .

Believe It or Not

Lesson B | More mysteries

1 GET READY TO READ

Unexplained phenomena

Have you ever witnessed an unexplained phenomenon or strange event? What happened?

A Read the two letters written to a science magazine.

B Now read the letters again along with the responses. Pay attention to the words in blue.

C Match each word in blue with its definition.

1. happening often or regularly: _____
2. prior, happening before: _____
3. break down, stop working: _____
4. saw or noticed something: _____
5. to cause something to happen: _____
6. guessed: _____
7. mysterious, hard to explain: _____
8. knowing or sensing something even though you don't have all the facts: _____

D Pair work. For each situation, circle two facts and underline one theory. Then, compare your answers with a partner. Which words helped you to decide which were facts and which were theories?

> ▶ **Ask & Answer**
>
> What do you think of the scientific explanations for each of the events in B? Do you think there could be other causes for each? What?

Ask the expert
This week's topic:

Unexplained Phenomena

My husband Max has an unusual problem: he **routinely** causes light bulbs, TVs, and computers to blow up when he's nearby. Even the batteries in his watch only last a week or so, and then they stop working. Do you have any idea what might **trigger** these events? For some **inexplicable** reason, they usually happen when my husband is stressed or upset about something. Do you have any idea what's going on?

Signed,
In the Dark

Dear In the Dark,

*Believe it or not, your husband's condition is not that uncommon. Although there's no definite evidence yet, some researchers have **speculated** that your husband's condition might be created by electronic impulses in the brain. This electricity somehow leaves the body and can cause electronic devices (like computers) to **malfunction.***

I saw a show on TV last night about an 11-year-old British girl who says she is able to recall her past life. The child said that in her **previous** life she was a nineteenth-century German farmer named Hans Treuter. The most amazing thing I **observed** was that when hypnotized, the child spoke fluent German (a language neither she nor her parents speak). My **intuition** tells me that this story isn't real, but I'd like to know what scientists have to say.

Signed,
Doubting Thomas

Dear Thomas,
You're right to question stories like these. Many scientists suspect that cases of past life recall may be due to an extraordinary memory. In other words, a person is able to remember in great detail something he or she has seen, heard, or read—even if this only happened very briefly, or when the person was very young.

A Pair work. Read the three facts at the beginning of the reading. Then skim the remainder of the passage. What may have been the cause of the disappearances? Tell your partner.

Mystery World

Consider the facts below:

1. Over the last twenty years, hundreds of cargo ships—many as big as a soccer field—have mysteriously disappeared or been destroyed in the North Atlantic and near the tip of South America and South Africa.

2. The Bermuda Triangle, roughly the area between southern Florida, Puerto Rico, and Bermuda, has been the site of many ship and aircraft disappearances over the last hundred years.

5 3. In the Pacific Ocean, just off the coast of central Japan, there is a region known as "The Devil's Sea" —given its name in 1955 after ten ships vanished. The area has been named a danger zone by the Japanese government for the number of ships that are routinely, and inexplicably, lost there.

For years, scientists struggled to explain these events. Many speculated that bad weather or machine malfunction were responsible. But now there is evidence that may shed new light on the disappearances. Satellites
10 set up by the European Space Agency have recently identified enormous waves far out in the oceans. These "rogue waves" are often nearly 30 meters high, or about the size of a twelve-story building. They often rise unexpectedly, like monstrous walls of water from the sea, crashing down with great force, and then, they disappear.

Though waves this size have been part of nautical* folklore for centuries, scientists believed that they were extremely rare (occurring only once every 10,000 years). The satellite data, though, proves that they are more
15 common than once thought. Scientists now also suspect that these waves may have been responsible for many of the unexplained disappearances of low-flying aircraft and ships over the years.

So, how and why do waves like these form? Until very recently, oceanographers** thought that rogues were the result of many smaller waves joining together to form a giant wave. But in analyzing the recent satellite images collected by the European Space Agency, scientists have noted that rogues appear to form most often in places
20 where waves of different strengths come together from different directions. At the southernmost tip of Africa, for example, where the Atlantic and Indian Oceans meet, it is quite common for waves to crash into each other. Combined with the strong ocean currents in the region, waves may then grow to enormous height. This theory may explain the occurrence of rogue waves in similar locations around the globe (such as at the tip of South America) known for colliding waves and strong ocean currents. However, it does not explain why the waves form in places
25 where there are no fast-moving ocean currents—such as in the North Sea.

To understand why rogue waves might form in places like the North Sea and other spots around the globe, oceanographers have turned to studying the weather and its effect on the ocean. Some scientists now believe that fast-moving winds blowing for long periods of time over waves in the open ocean might create a rogue monster. However, this has been observed most often in the southern oceans, and still does not fully explain why huge waves
30 form in places like the North Sea. Still, scientists are hoping that by studying weather patterns they may be able to predict where rogue waves are likely to develop.

Though scientists are beginning to understand more about rogue waves, there is still a lot to learn. However, now that it is clear that these waves are more common than once thought, efforts are being made to improve ships' safety and to minimize the loss of life.

35 *nautical: related to sailing and the sea   **oceanographers: scientists who study the oceans

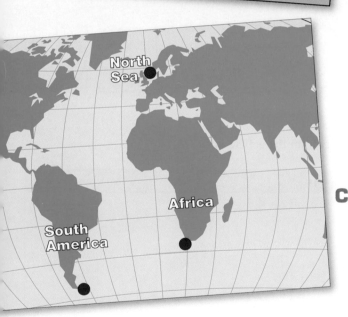

B Complete the sentences below with the appropriate words or phrases from the article.

_____ 1. Ships and aircraft have _____ in areas such as the _____ , the Bermuda Triangle, and the _____.

_____ 2. It's possible that bad weather or _____ were responsible for these disappearances.

_____ 3. Recently, _____ identified enormous waves far out in the oceans that are nearly _____ high.

_____ 4. Although scientists once believed that the waves happened only _____ years, it is now clear that they are more _____ than once thought.

_____ 5. Scientists now suspect that the _____ may have been caused by these waves.

_____ 6. Rogue waves seem to happen in places, such as _____ and _____ where waves of different _____ come together from _____.

_____ 7. It's also possible that these enormous waves are also caused by _____.

_____ 8. Even though there is a lot that scientists still don't understand about rogue waves, shipping companies are now trying to _____.

C Read the statements in B and decide if each is a fact or a theory. Write the correct letter (*For T*) next to each statement above.

Distinguishing fact from theory
A fact is something that can be checked and proven. A theory is a possible explanation for something. When discussing a theory, speculative words and phrases are often used such as:

may	*might*	*could*
It seems/appears . . .	*It's possible . . .*	
We suspect . . .	*We think/believe . . .*	

▶ **Ask & Answer**

Name another "unexplained phenomenon" (e.g., ghosts, UFOs) that you know of. How could it be explained?

D Pair work. Close your book. Summarize the article with a partner. Include something you learned from the reading that surprised you.

A Read the article below.

FIRST AT THE ROOF OF THE WORLD *by Michelle Gao*

Tibet is one of the coldest inhabited places on Earth, with winter temperatures plunging as low as -40 degrees Celsius. Until very recently, scientists believed that the first inhabitants of Tibet arrived only around 4,000 years ago, after the end of its most recent Ice Age. They theorized that previously the Tibetan plateau had been covered by ice a mile thick.

Then, in 1986, a researcher from Hong Kong University named David Zhang made a remarkable discovery. High on a mountain slope, about 85 km from the city of Lhasa, he found 19 human handprints and footprints, embedded in ancient rock at the edge of a hot spring. But the real surprise didn't come until 1999. That's when he and his colleagues tried a technique called optical dating, which revealed that the prints were actually more than 20,000 years old.

Zhang determined that the handprints and footprints were made by six different people, two of them children. He also found the remains of a stove there. It seems likely that this group of early Tibetans came to the hot spring to take refuge from the extreme cold of th Ice Age. Zhang says "The findings mean that human settlement occured here 16,000 years earlier than scientists had thought, and also that human beings had the ability to adapt to such a cold environment."

But why did they press their hands and feet into the mud? Zhang thinks they did it out of curiosity, or maybe just for fun. The soft mud around the spring preserved the prints when it later turned into a form of stone called travertine. In the future, Zhang hopes to explor further on the Tibetan Plateau to collect more evidence of early Tibetan settlements.

B Review the expressions used to distinguish fact from theory on page 59.
Then complete the chart with brief notes about theories and facts from the article in **A**.

Facts	Theories

C Complete a summary of the article in **A**. Include at least three facts and three theories.

An article entitled "First at the Roof of the World," by Michelle Gao, discusses . . .

Writing a summary

A summary is a written condensation of the most important points in a text in your own words. You can rearrange or reorganize the ideas to make them clearer. As a general rule, you should not copy more than five words in a row from the text.

D Pair work. Exchange summaries with your partner and locate the facts and theories. Are all the most important points included?

4 COMMUNICATION

Activity 1: The sixth sense

A The "sixth sense" is often defined as a strong hunch (feeling) that a person has about something or someone. Read about one mother's experience.

I HAD A HUNCH . . .

Kathy Sansano arrived home from work two months ago at 7:00 in the evening. "Normally, my husband is home before me, but when I got in, his briefcase was there, but he wasn't," recalls Sansano. She just assumed that he went to the store for something. Sansano began preparing dinner, but couldn't shake the feeling that something was wrong. "I just started feeling very anxious and had to sit down. Five minutes later my husband phoned to say that our son had been injured in a football game at school."

Luckily, the boy only suffered a broken wrist, but Sansano still can't explain how she knew something was wrong. "It might have been 'mother's intuition,'" she laughs. "My son and I have always been very close."

Science identifies five basic senses that humans use to experience the world. There is now evidence that humans may also possess a sixth sense—or an intuition about people or events. Recent studies done suggest that insects and animals release odorless chemicals called pheromones into the environment to signal emotions such as fear or aggression. When another creature of the same species senses the chemical (via its nose), a certain behavior is triggered in that creature; for example, it will prepare to fight or to protect itself.

Scientists believe that humans long ago may have communicated using these kinds of chemical signals, and that we continue to produce and sense pheromones, although less than our ancestors did. It has been described this way: "How often do we hear someone say, for example, 'I walked into the room, and something just didn't seem right.'" It may be that the person is sensing chemical messages that have been produced by others—even if those individuals are no longer present. Kathy Sansano's husband may have left the house feeling afraid and worried about their son. When Kathy got home, she sensed his anxiety—which may explain the unease she then experienced.

B Pair work. Was Kathy Sansano's hunch just a coincidence or does the article suggest another possibility? Discuss your ideas with a partner.

Activity 2: Have any of these things ever happened to you?

A Look at the list below. Choose one, or think of something else that happened to you that you couldn't explain.

- I had a feeling that something was going to happen, and then it did.
- I had a dream that something was going to happen, and it came true.
- I started thinking about a person, and then he or she called or came to visit me.

B Group work. Get into a group of four people. Tell your group the story of what happened to you. Your group listens and asks you questions. Then, each person in your group offers a possible explanation for the event.

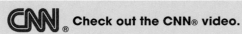 **Check out the CNN® video.** **Practice your English online at elt.heinle.com/worldpass**

Unit 5: Believe It or Not

A Study the word combinations in the box. Write the letter of the word combination with a meaning similar to that of the underlined phrase after each sentence below.

> **Word combinations with *mystery***
>
> a. It's a mystery to me.　　　　　　d. a murder mystery
> b. solve/unravel a mystery　　　　e. the mystery deepens.
> c. give someone an air of mystery　f. a complete/total mystery

1. We still don't know what happened to Jim Thompson. Every year, <u>we understand it less</u>. ___
2. <u>I have absolutely no idea</u> how that bird got into my apartment! ___
3. I like to relax by reading <u>a detective novel about a killing</u>, but I can never figure out who committed the crime. ___
4. I don't know how birds find their way when they migrate. It's <u>something I can't understand</u>. ___
5. Her exotic clothes and unusual accent <u>made the woman seem unusual and interesting</u>. ___
6. It took three years of hard work by police detectives to <u>figure out what happened</u> in the case of the missing baby. ___

B Use your dictionary to help you add these nouns to the correct group.

> sleuth　　　　clue　　　　puzzle　　　　speculation
> investigator　　enigma　　　evidence　　　hypothesis

1. proof, information, _____, _____
2. detective, researcher, _____, _____
3. question, mystery, _____, _____
4. theory, guess, _____, _____

Incorrect: *My wife is having three cats.*　　　　**Correct:** *My wife <u>has</u> three cats.*

C Find the best noun for each verb.

1. We solve ___.
2. We answer ___.
3. We find ___.
4. We catch ___.
5. We state ___.

a. a solution
b. a question
c. a fact
d. a mystery
e. a criminal

D The prefix *mal-* means "bad." Complete the sentences with a word from the box.
Check the meaning in your dictionary if necessary.

malfunction	malnourished	malpractice
maltreat	malcontent	malformed

1. Cheryl is a real _____. She's always unhappy with everything at the office, but she complains every time they try to change something!
2. The doctor lost his job because of _____ . He made some very serious mistakes with medication, and almost killed two patients.
3. The plane crash was caused by a _____ in the plane's electronic system.
4. The newspaper had sad photos of skinny, _____ children who were suffering from the famine.
5. My little brother was born with a _____ foot, but the surgery was successful and now he can walk without problems.
6. The dog's previous owner used to _____ him, so now he's afraid of people.

In Other Words

A theory is a possible explanation for something that has reasons behind it: *Scientists have a theory that the dinosaurs disappeared because of climate change.*
A guess is an attempt to say what is true or what will happen without knowing exactly: *My guess is that many people will be absent from class tomorrow.*
If you have a hunch about something, you have a feeling or intuition about it: *I have a hunch you'll find your missing wallet at home.*

If you search for something, you look for it very systematically and carefully: *An airplane searched for any sign of the missing boat.*
Look for is a more general term: *I'm looking for Anne / my keys / a better job.*
Hunt for is informal and means look around in a large area: *The kids hunted for shells on the beach.*

 **Watch out!** **adopt and adapt**
Don't confuse these two very similar verbs. *Adopt* means to take legal responsibility for a child: *Mr. and Mrs. Lee adopted a little girl.* *Adapt* means to change something to make it suitable: *The movie was adapted for a TV series.*

1 VOCABULARY FOCUS

Trends in the workplace

 One trend in the workplace is that more people are telecommuting than before. Another trend is that people are working with flexible schedules. Can you think of other trends?

A Read what these people are saying about trends or issues in business today.
Match each person to the item they are talking about.

☐ fair treatment of women   ☐ downsizing (reducing staff)   ☐ mail-order businesses

1. Jerome

I got my first job two years ago and then there was a downturn in the economy. Just my luck! First, my employer cut back on production. Then, when there wasn't enough work to go around, they started laying off people. About half of my coworkers had to find new jobs! My friends tell me I should look for a new job. Others tell me I should stick with this company for a while longer. I can't figure out what to do!

2. Linda

Let's face it—in the workplace, women still don't have the same opportunities as men. I've worked for the same company for ten years. I got passed over for a promotion last year. I found out the job went to a younger man with less experience. I handed in my notice last week and I feel good about quitting. I'm going back to school for an MBA. Will it help me get ahead in my next job? Who knows? One thing is certain: I'm not going to give up until I get what I want—equal treatment at work.

3. Kristin

In today's business climate, you've got to be clever—come up with ideas that others haven't thought of yet. Take my friend Anezka, an organic apple farmer. Five years ago, her business wasn't making a profit. It was about to go under. Then organic fruit really caught on. Suddenly it seemed that everyone wanted to buy her organic apples! She then decided to try something new: She set up a mail-order business so her customers could order her apples from home and get them quickly. Sales took off and Anezka made even more money. Now she's thinking about retiring early.

B Look at the expressions in **A**. Match them with their definitions. Which ones are used in a positive way? Which ones are used in a negative or neutral way?

1. cut back on __c__
2. lay off ____
3. stick with ____
4. figure out ____
5. pass over ____
6. find out ____
7. hand in ____
8. get ahead ____
9. give up ____
10. come up with ____
11. go under ____
12. catch on ____
13. set up ____
14. take off ____

a. go bankrupt
b. not notice; ignore
c. decrease
d. increase dramatically
e. stop trying
f. continue
g. discover
h. stop employing someone
i. become popular
j. understand or solve
k. think of
l. give to someone
m. be successful
n. organize and start

2 LISTENING

Pretending to work

> Do you ever goof off at school or work?
> What do you usually do to avoid working or studying?

A David and Marc are being interviewed about a book that was recently published in France. Listen and complete the information about the book. (CD Tracks 19 & 20)

Author: _Corinne Maier_
Name of the book in English: _____
What the book is about: _____

_____

What kind of book is it: ☐ self-help   ☐ historical fiction   ☐ satire

Real English
goof off = to waste time and avoid working

B Which statements would David agree with?
Which ones would Marc agree with? Circle your answers.

David
1. We go to work because it's necessary.   Yes   No
2. Most readers can't understand the book.   Yes   No
3. The book was very funny.   Yes   No

Marc
1. The book had a positive tone.   Yes   No
2. The book encourages people not to try hard at work.   Yes   No

A. Read the sentences below. What do you think each underlined phrase means?

1. We didn't budget enough money and had to <u>get by</u> on only $20 a day.
2. Roberto was sick and <u>got behind</u> at work.
3. You need an employee ID to <u>get into</u> the building.
4. We were so busy we couldn't <u>get away</u> from the office until midnight.
5. I'm busy now. Can I <u>get back to</u> you later today?

B. Now complete the sentences below using the correct form of the underlined phrases above.

1. Let's drive out Third Avenue so that we can _____ from all this traffic.
2. If we wait to buy tickets until later, we may not be able to _____ the theater.
3. The airline lost my suitcase and I had to _____ with just the clothes I had.
4. The travel agent promised to _____ us later today with information about flights.
5. Bill _____ on his credit card payments, and now he owes the bank over $5,000.

◀)) **C** Pair work. Listen again. What tips does the author give? Complete each one below. Would you do each one? Why or why not? Explain to a partner. (CD Track 21)

1. <u>Pretend</u> to be a smoker.
2. Hide a _____ inside a work _____.
3. Be nice to _____ workers.
4. Never accept a position of _____.
5. Go for the most _____ position.
6. _____.
7. _____.

▶ **Ask & Answer**

What do you think of Corinne Maier's opinions about work? Do you agree or disagree with her ideas? Why?

D Pair work. Add one or two tips to the list in C. Then share your ideas with another pair.

> *You should pretend to be sick. That way you can take a lot of time off.*

3 LANGUAGE FOCUS

Phrasal verbs

A These coworkers are talking about their company and its advertising plan. Read their statements. Underline six more phrasal verbs.

> *In this economic climate, a lot of companies are <u>going under</u>. I'm worried that our company, too, will go bankrupt and will have to <u>lay off</u> some staff.*

> *I don't think we should make any drastic changes. Let's stick with our current strategy.*

> *We need to set up a marketing research team. The team should then come up with some new ideas for an ad campaign.*

Understanding phrasal verbs

A phrasal verb is a group of words, usually a verb + particle such as *give up*, used as a verb. The particle *(up)* looks like a preposition but functions as part of the verb. Note the difference in meaning below:
give = offer something
give up = quit or stop doing something

> *Well, even though times are tough, we shouldn't cut back on our advertising budget.*

> *No, that sounds like we're giving up. I'm sure we can figure out a solution.*

B A transitive verb takes an object. An intransitive verb does not. Decide if each phrasal verb in A is transitive or intransitive. If it is transitive, circle the object. Then write the phrasal verbs in the correct column below.

Transitive verb	Object	Intransitive verb
lay off	some staff	going under

C Rewrite the sentences below using the phrasal verbs in the box.

carry out	come up with	hand in	pass over	think about
~~catch on~~	get ahead	hang on	put off	

1. Do you think this style will <u>become popular</u> next season?   <u>Do you think this style will catch on next season?</u>

2. It's impossible to <u>succeed</u> in this competitive world. _____

3. I <u>submitted</u> the final version of my proposal yesterday. _____

4. Are you <u>considering</u> hiring him? _____

5. She was <u>not chosen</u> for the new position. _____

6. In my new job, I have to <u>perform</u> many challenging tasks. _____

7. We'll have to <u>postpone</u> the meeting until next week. _____

8. Can you <u>think of</u> any new ideas? _____

9. If I can <u>wait</u> until the summer, I'll get a long break then. _____

D Group work. Get into a group of three people and work together on this problem.
Use the phrasal verbs in the box (and others of your own) to answer the questions.

carry out	come up with	set up	think about	catch on	figure out	take off

You work for an ice cream company that is about to go under. You desperately need to come up with a new flavor to win back customers. Discuss these questions and use the phrasal verbs in the box for your discussion.

1. What is the name of the new flavor? _____
2. How will you sell it? _____
3. Where will you sell it? _____
4. Who are your target customers? _____
5. What is your advertising slogan? _____

> *To test the new flavor, we could set up a booth in the mall and give away samples . . .*

> *We need to come up with an effective way to advertise the new flavor.*

E Class activity. Present your idea to the class. Vote on the best idea.

World Link

While vanilla and chocolate are the most popular flavors of ice cream, other more interesting flavors are found around the world. Ice creams flavored with fish, orchids, and chicken wings are offered in Japan. And a restaurant in California even features garlic-flavored ice cream! Yum . . . ?

I can agree to that.

A Pair work. Janet and her boss are solving a problem at work. Read the conversation and answer the questions that follow. Compare your answers with a partner.

Negotiating a solution

Mr. Blair: Janet, I need you to present the sales report on Monday.

Janet: You do? But that's not possible. Today is Thursday, and I usually spend a week writing it!

Mr. Blair: I know. But I just found out that our new company president will be arriving from New York at 9:00. And you have to remember that this will be his first visit to our office. Would you consider working on Saturday if I give you the day off on Tuesday?

Janet: I'm afraid I can't. My sister's wedding is this Saturday.

Mr. Blair: Well, bear in mind that the sales meeting is the first thing on Monday morning now.

Janet: Hmm. I have an idea. If you'll let two other people work with me today, I could put the report together tomorrow.

Mr. Blair: OK, I can agree to that. Rick and Sandy can help you.

Janet: And maybe your assistant could make the photocopies?

Mr. Blair: That will be fine.

Janet: OK, then . . . I'd better get to work!

1. What does Mr. Blair want?   2. What does Janet want?   3. What agreement do they make?

B Complete the boxes with the expressions the speakers used for these things.

Bargaining	Bringing in facts
Would you consider . . . if I . . . ?	Bear in mind that . . .
_____	_____
Accepting	**Refusing**
_____	_____
_____	_____

C Pair work. Choose a role and plan what you will say. Then work with your partner to reach an agreement.

Role #1:
You are a coffee shop owner who wants to keep costs down
- The price of coffee has gone up
- A new coffee shop in the neighborhood could put you out of business
- You are planning to expand the shop and need to cut down on costs

Role #2:
You are a coffee shop employee who wants a raise (decide how much)
- You work 6 A.M.–2 P.M.–the busiest time
- You haven't had a raise in two years
- The new coffee shop pays its employees more
- You've come up with some very popular new dishes and sales have taken off

D Pair work. Negotiate a solution to the situation below and role-play it with your partner.

Student A: You want to go away this weekend with your friends to relax and have fun.

Student B: You are Student A's brother/sister. You want him or her to stay home and help get ready for a big family party.

Today's Workplace

| *Lesson B* | Job choices |

1 GET READY TO READ

What do you want to be when you grow up?

 When you were a child what did you want to be when you grew up? Did your ideas change?

A Children and teenagers at schools around New York City were asked by a local news magazine, "What do you want to be when you grow up?" Read what they said.

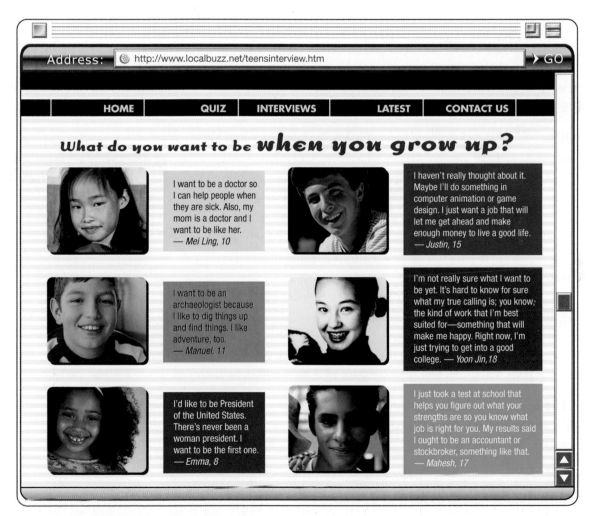

Address: http://www.localbuzz.net/teensinterview.htm → GO

HOME   QUIZ   INTERVIEWS   LATEST   CONTACT US

What do you want to be when you grow up?

I want to be a doctor so I can help people when they are sick. Also, my mom is a doctor and I want to be like her.
— *Mei Ling, 10*

I haven't really thought about it. Maybe I'll do something in computer animation or game design. I just want a job that will let me get ahead and make enough money to live a good life.
— *Justin, 15*

I want to be an archaeologist because I like to dig things up and find things. I like adventure, too.
— *Manuel, 11*

I'm not really sure what I want to be yet. It's hard to know for sure what my true calling is; you know, the kind of work that I'm best suited for—something that will make me happy. Right now, I'm just trying to get into a good college. — *Yoon Jin, 18*

I'd like to be President of the United States. There's never been a woman president. I want to be the first one.
— *Emma, 8*

I just took a test at school that helps you figure out what your strengths are so you know what job is right for you. My results said I ought to be an accountant or stockbroker, something like that.
— *Mahesh, 17*

B Pair work. Answer the questions below with a partner.

1. What does each young person want to be?
2. How are the responses similar?
3. How are they different?
4. Yoon Jin says, "It's hard to know for sure what my true calling is . . . " What does she mean by "true calling"?
5. Which of the others seems to know his or her true calling? Explain your answer.

C Pair work. Do you know what your true calling is? Discuss your ideas with your partner.

A Skim the interview on page 71. Then complete the sentence below.

The interview with Cristina Resende is mainly about _____.

a. her goal to become the president of a technology company
b. her plans for traveling throughout the Mediterranean region
c. her desire to buy and run a small store in her neighborhood

B Find the information that completes these sentences.

1. Cristina believes her true calling is _____.
2. She didn't pursue this dream when she was younger because _____.
3. Cristina's current occupations are _____.
4. Cristina found out about The Mediterranean after _____.
5. Cristina was nervous the day she asked to work at The Mediterranean because _____.
6. In three months Cristina is going to _____.

C Pair work. Who do you think said each statement below? Write the person's name. Underline the information in the reading you used to make your choice. Then compare your answers with a partner.

1. ___Cristina___ "The experience I've gained in the business world has prepared me to manage a store."
2. _____ "Why would you quit your job as a manager to run a deli? There's no stability in that!"
3. _____ "I know she loves food, but I wasn't sure at first why she wanted to work at The Mediterranean."
4. _____ "I'm glad that someone I trust is going to take over The Mediterranean."
5. _____ "I'm sure you'll do great! I wish I could quit my job and pursue my dream."

> **Reminder: Inferencing**
>
> Information is not always stated directly. Often a reader must infer, or make guesses about something, using the information that is available in the reading.

D Pair work. Reread the interview and find the expressions below. What do you think each one means? Write a short definition, and then compare your ideas with a partner.

1. (line 45) an opportunity in disguise _____
2. (line 48) I had butterflies in my stomach _____
3. (line 56) so to speak _____
4. (line 86) come around _____

E Pair work. Discuss the situations below with a partner.

1. Have you, or someone you know, ever been offered an opportunity in disguise?
2. Talk about a time that you had butterflies in your stomach.
3. Have you ever come around to something you didn't like at first?

> ▶ **Ask & Answer**
>
> What do you think is the best way to find your true calling in life?

Your True Calling

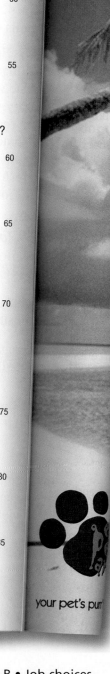

Do you ever find yourself thinking, "What exactly do I want to do with my life?" Tim Warner interviews Cristina Resende, a 32-year-old businesswoman who has recently found a way to pursue her true calling.

5 **Interviewer:** Why don't we start off by talking a little about how you developed your interest in food and cooking.

Resende: Well, food has always been my passion. As a child, I used to love preparing meals with my grandmother, who was from Brazil. And as I got older, I spent a lot of time in the kitchen, experimenting with different dishes—Thai soups, German tortes, Italian pastas.

15 **Interviewer:** But you never considered a career in the culinary arts?

Resende: Not at all. You know, as a kid, I grew up learning that a person went to college and got a job in business, law, or something like that. Telling my parents that I wanted to "study food" would've been impossible. They never would have agreed.

25 **Interviewer:** So, fast forward to the present. You're now a business development manager for an international technology company. It doesn't exactly sound like the career you dreamed of. Tell us, how did The Mediterranean come into your life?

30 **Resende:** About three years ago, I moved into an apartment around the corner from this store—it's a lovely little place that specializes in imported food from Greece, Spain, and Italy. There's a deli as well. Anyway, I'd drop in there once a week or so to pick up different items. But the next thing you know, I was talking with the owner, Alex Kanellos, about a cheese or a certain wine. Then one day, he jokingly suggested that I work in the deli since I had all of these ideas. I just laughed when he said it, but when I got home, I couldn't stop thinking that maybe this part-time job was an opportunity in disguise.

Interviewer: So you took the job?

Resende: Oh yeah. I went to the deli the next morning. I had butterflies in my stomach. I kept thinking . . . I'm thirty years old and I'm taking a part-time job 50 in a deli. What am I doing? [laughs] When I asked Mr. Kanellos if he was serious about letting me work there part-time, he looked a little surprised at first. But then, Mr. Kanellos handed me 55 an apron, and the rest is history, so to speak. I've been working there every Saturday for the last couple of years.

Interviewer: What led to your decision to buy the deli?

Resende: About eight months ago, Mr. Kanellos 60 mentioned that he was getting ready to retire, and was going to sell the place. So, I started thinking . . . if he's going to sell it to someone, why not me? When I approached Mr. Kanellos with the idea, 65 he was very open to it. I also think he was pleased to turn over the place to someone he knew.

Interviewer: And what about your job with the tech company? 70

Resende: I'm going to stay for another three months, until Mr. Kanellos retires.

Interviewer: How are your family and friends reacting to the news?

Resende: My friends are really happy for me. A lot 75 of them have jobs they can't stand—especially my friend Suki—and most would love to make a change in their lives. My boyfriend has been pretty supportive, too, though at first, he 80 thought I was crazy to work part-time at the deli. My mom isn't thrilled, though. She's worried about me leaving a "good job" to run the store, but I know that as a small businesswoman, I can be 85 successful, too. I'm sure she'll come around!

your pet's pur

A Pair work. Read the job listing and then the cover letter below. Discuss with your partner why Dale Sanford thinks he is qualified for the job.

> **Animal care specialist**
>
> National Zoo requires experienced person to feed, water, and clean the cages of small animals. Duties also include conducting tours for young visitors. Send résumé and cover letter to Cassandra Beck, National Zoo, P.O. Box 42, Metropolis City MA 02210

980 Wilson Drive
Metropolis City MA 02203

Ms. Cassandra Beck
National Zoo
P.O. Box 42
Metropolis City MA 02210

Dear Ms. Beck:

I'm writing to apply for the position that was advertised in the Metropolis Daily News. My background makes me very well-qualified to be an animal care specialist. I will graduate next month from Pacific University with a degree in biology and have taken several courses in animal behavior. During my summer vacations, I worked in the office of a local veterinarian and helped to care for a variety of animals, including dogs, cats, snakes, and birds. I am also a volunteer for Save the Animals, a local rescue group. My own pets include two dogs, a rabbit, and a turtle, all adopted through Save the Animals. My résumé is enclosed. Thank you very much for your consideration, and I look forward to hearing from you.

Sincerely,
Dale Sanford
Dale Sanford

B Pair work. In the body of the letter, underline the purpose of the letter. Circle Dale's qualifications for the job. Then discuss these questions with a partner.

1. What information is included in the first sentence of the letter?
2. Do you think Dale is qualified for the job?

C Choose one of the job listings below and write a cover letter to apply for the job. Include your purpose for writing the letter and at least three qualifications that make you right for the job.

International Tour Guide Tour leaders needed for our small-group luxury tours to Hawaii, South America, and East Asia. Excellent salary and benefits, plus unlimited free travel. Contact Melinda Lee, Starline Travel, 16 Bayfield Drive, Mayfield, NY 22267

Personal shopper Gracy's Department Store is looking for people with a great sense of style to help our customers plan their wardrobes. Competitive salary plus great employee discounts on all our clothes. Contact Personnel Dept., P.O. Box 401, San Francisco CA 61240

D Pair work. Exchange letters with a partner. Make two suggestions to improve your partner's letter.

Activity 1: Appointment with a career counselor

A Pair work. Interview your partner using the questions below.

1. What are (or were) your favorite subjects in school? _____
2. What are three things that really make you happy? _____
3. What skills or talents do you have? What things are you good at doing? List at least two.
   _____   _____
4. How would you finish this sentence?
   I prefer to . . .
   ☐ work on my own.   ☐ work as a member of a team.   ☐ manage a group of people.
5. What is most important to you in a career? Rank each of the following from 1 to 3.
   (1 = not important   2 = somewhat important   3 = very important)

   ☐ money   ☐ freedom to be my own boss

   ☐ intellectual challenge   ☐ helping others

   ☐ a flexible schedule   ☐ company perks (e.g., gym membership, day care for children)

   ☐ a good retirement package   ☐ a creative environment

   ☐ the ability to travel   ☐ other _____

B Pair work. Look at the answers your partner gave you in A. What career(s) do you think your partner is best suited for? Why? Choose from the list below or come up with your own ideas.

tour guide	DJ	yoga instructor	professional shopper	firefighter	doctor or nurse
decorator	lawyer	private investigator	scientist	chef	carpenter
engineer	taxi driver	game programmer	jewelry designer	coach	editor

Activity 2: Try to see things my way

A Pair work. Assume one of the roles below. With your partner, try to reach an agreement about what to do by the end of your conversation.

Student A: You're a senior in college majoring in business. You've decided to give up your studies and drop out of school to pursue your true calling in life, which you believe is a career in music. To begin your new life as a musician, you need to borrow some money. You decide to talk to a parent. Explain your plans and try to get your parent to come around to your way of thinking.

Student B: You're Student A's parent. You are against your child's plans. You think your son or daughter is making a very serious mistake and is going to throw his or her life away by dropping out of school and becoming a musician. You think your child should complete his or her studies and put off doing anything in music until after graduation.

B Group work. Perform your role play for another pair.

 Check out the CNN® video. **Practice your English online at elt.heinle.com/worldpass**

Unit 6: Today's Workplace

A Study the word combinations in the box. Then complete the sentences, using the correct form of the phrase.

> **More word combinations with *get***
>
> *get off* = leave from work; be released from something without penalty
> *get into* = become involved in; enter
> *get behind* = support
> *get around* = avoid (usually doing something)
> *get around to* = do something eventually, often after procrastinating
> *get along with* = be compatible with
> *get together* = meet informally

1. Let's get _____ at the coffee shop some time next week, OK?
2. In her speech, the mayor urged citizens to get _____ the city's clean-up campaign.
3. I got _____ holiday crowds last year by ordering presents over the Internet.
4. Kayla got _____ surfing while she was on vacation in Hawaii. She loves it.
5. I'd always wanted to plant a garden, and I finally got _____ it last year.
6. Ray just doesn't get _____ his boss. They argue a lot.
7. Would you like to meet me after work? I get _____ at 6:30 tonight.

B Circle the term that doesn't fit. Use your dictionary as necessary.

1. salary   wages   paycheck   bills
2. boss   supervisor   intern   manager
3. out of work   layoff   unemployed   take off
4. application   calling   ambition   goal
5. get ahead   successful   profitable   go under
6. come up with   invent   give up   make
7. career   customer   job   position
8. give up   stick with   continue   keep on

> **I didn't know that!**
> In ancient Rome, soldiers received a handful of salt every day to use on their food. After a while, this was replaced by money to buy salt. The payment was called *salarium* in Latin (meaning "salt money").
> Later, in several European languages, *salary* became a word for any kind of pay for work.

C Match these sentences with their uses.

1. Everything will work out. ___
2. Get to work! ___
3. We can work it out. ___
4. You have your work cut out for you. ___
5. It's in the works. ___
6. Don't get all worked up about it. (informal) ___

a. used to say that people can make an agreement
b. used to say that a project will be very difficult
c. used to tell someone not to get upset about something
d. used to say that a situation will be OK
e. used to tell someone to stop being lazy
f. used to say that something is being planned or prepared

D Complete the conversations with one of the sentences from C.

1. A: Mom, why are you yelling at me?
   B: I told you to clean your room, but you haven't. _____!

2. A: Maybe we should break up . . . I love you, but we just argue all the time.
   B: But I don't want to stop seeing you! _____.

3. A: What are we going to have to eat at our party? I don't have any time to cook!
   B: Don't worry. I asked everyone to bring snacks. _____.

4. A: Julio said he would call me last night, and I waited up until midnight!
   B: _____. He probably just forgot.

5. A: I'm going to be designing and maintaining the company's new web site.
   B: Wow, _____! That's a big job.

6. A: When will you be transferred to the New York office?
   B: I'm not sure yet, but my boss told me _____.

E What do these scientists study? Match the columns. Then circle the job that would be most interesting for you.

1. An oceanographer studies ____.   a. plants
2. An astronomer studies ____.   b. animals
3. A psychologist studies ____.   c. ancient civilizations
4. A meteorologist studies ____.   d. the weather
5. A zoologist studies ____.   e. the sea
6. A botanist studies ____.   f. the earth and rocks
7. A geologist studies ____.   g. the human mind
8. An archaeologist studies ____.   h. space

In Other Words

Company is a general term for a business organization that makes or sells things: *Sony is a Japanese company.*
A **business** can be large or small: *My sister has her own business—she's a hairdresser.*
A **firm** is a business of professionals: *Claudia works for a big accounting firm.*
A **corporation** is a large business with special legal status: *I have fifty shares of stock in that corporation.*

To **succeed** means to achieve your goals: *Her ambition was to become a pilot, and she succeeded.*
Make it is an informal expression for succeed in a profession: *It's really hard to make it as a new actor in Hollywood.*
If you are **doing well**, you are successful in work or education: *My brother's company is doing very well. / My son is studying at Oxford University, and he's doing very well.*
If you **thrive on** something, it motivates or energizes you to succeed: *Athletes thrive on competition.*

staff
Staff is a collective noun (similar to *team, faculty,* or *family*). It refers to the whole group of workers and is uncountable. To refer to one person, use *staff member.*
   Our company sent three staff members to the conference.
   Our company sent three ~~staffs~~ to the conference.

Review: Units 4–6

1 LANGUAGE CHECK

Circle the correct answer.

1. Last year, I didn't have my driver's license yet,
   so I ____ drive my dad's new car.
   a. mustn't   b. couldn't   c. didn't have to

2. It's raining hard. Let's put ___ the picnic until next week.
   a. up   b. off   c. in

3. The car was completely destroyed in the crash.
   The driver ____ been going very fast.
   a. must have   b. can't have   c. may not have

4. I came up ___ a great idea for redecorating my living room.
   a. over   b. with   c. across

5. I waited for an hour, but my friends didn't show up.
   I think I ____ made a mistake about the date.
   a. couldn't have   b. should have   c. may have

6. Dina didn't study but she got a good grade.
   That class ____ been very difficult!
   a. must have   b. might have   c. couldn't have

7. In my opinion, if you like Denise,
   you ____ call her and ask her out on a date.
   a. could   b. should   c. must

8. I brought a raincoat and an umbrella with me,
   but the weather was good, so I ____ use them.
   a. was required to   b. didn't have to   c. wasn't permitted

9. I didn't hear my cell phone ring. I ___ turned it on.
   a. must not have   b. could have   c. should not have

10. I stayed up all night working, and I handed
    ___ my report to my professor today.
    a. in   b. out   c. ahead

11. During the exam, we were ____ to put all our books
    and papers on the floor.
    a. chosen   b. required   c. needed

12. You have to work really hard if you want to get
    ____ in the software industry.
    a. ahead   b. over   c. about

2 VOCABULARY CHECK

Complete the sentences with words from the box, adding articles (*a, an*) as necessary. You will NOT use all of the words.

incident	theory	visionary	seemingly	evidence	documents
generation	witness	circumstances	apathetic	issue	motivated

1. Many people in the _____ born after 1990 don't know life without the Internet.

2. Don't be so _____ about global warming! If we don't take action, every living thing could be harmed.

3. Scientists have _____ that the dinosaurs died out because of climate change.

4. Improving public transportation is an important _____ in my city.

5. There is no _____ that Jim Thompson was eaten by a jungle tiger.

6. Many young people are very _____ and really work to improve the world we live in.

7. Investigators found a box of _____ that showed that the bank president had been stealing money from customers' accounts.

8. Older people in my country grew up in very different _____. The roads were poor and communication was difficult.

9. The new president is facing a _____ impossible task: reducing the high rate of unemployment in the country.

10. There was _____ in which two boys started fighting in the classroom.

3 NOW YOU'RE TALKING!

Situation 1

Situation 2

Situation 3

A Pair work. Choose one of the pictures and imagine yourselves in the situation. What would the people talk about? Briefly review the language notes from Units 4–6.

B Pair work. Read the statements in C and add two of your own goals. Then role-play the situation you chose keeping your speaking goals in mind.

C Now rate your speaking. Use + for good, ✓ for OK, and – for things you need to improve.

How did you do?	
I spoke loudly enough for my partner(s) to hear me.	
I spoke without too much hesitation.	
I spoke at a good rate of speed—not too fast or too slow.	
I used new vocabulary from the units.	
I used at least three expressions from the units.	
I practiced the grammar from the units.	
My own goals: 1. _____ 2. _____	

Does Crime Pay?

1 VOCABULARY FOCUS
Crossing the line

 If you found a diamond ring in the street, would you keep it or turn it in to the police?

A What do you think about doing these things? Rank them as 1 (not bad at all), 2 (kind of bad), or 3 (a serious crime).

- ☐ buying illegal CDs or DVDs on the street
- ☐ cheating on your taxes
- ☐ finding a large amount of money and keeping it
- ☐ making personal calls at work

- ☐ reading an entire magazine without buying it
- ☐ selling a concert ticket to a friend for double the original price
- ☐ taking your own food into a movie theater

B Pair work. Answer the questions below.

1. Would you ever do any of the things in A? Why or not?
2. Is anyone ever hurt in the above situations? If so, who? How are they hurt?

C Read about hacker John Draper and four people's reactions to what he did. Notice the words in blue.

Famous Hackers in History

In the early 1970s no one had heard of "phone phreaking" before. That was about to change. In 1972, two blind teenagers showed computer wiz John Draper how to hack into the phone system by using a toy whistle from a cereal box. The whistle's tone told the phone company's computer to stop charging the caller even though the call hadn't ended. John Draper used the whistle and taught others how to use it to make free long-distance telephone calls. He was caught in a few months, but didn't serve jail time for his first **offense**. He was arrested again in 1976 and this time **imprisoned** for five months.

John Draper now works in a **legitimate** job, running his own computer security firm. He and his **colleagues** create systems to stop computer viruses and spam (unwelcome e-mail) for their clients.

Since the 1970s, there have been **fundamental** changes to the law regarding hackers. They are now treated more harshly than John Draper was.

Jenny:	I don't know if Mr. Draper should've been **punished** with jail time or not. I think it's a gray area—on the one hand, no one got hurt directly, but the phone company surely lost money.
Chul Soo:	It's **outrageous** that he could've used a little plastic toy to cheat the phone system. The phone company should have better security than that.
Carlos:	He didn't **get away with** his crime. He has learned from his experience because he's no longer breaking the law. It's good that he's now helping people.
Zehra:	What he did was **illegal**—there's no doubt about that. He should've stayed **behind bars** longer than five months.

D Replace the underlined words below with one of the expressions from C.

1. Should they be <u>put in jail</u> or just given a fine? __imprisoned__
2. Draper is now engaged in business activities that are <u>allowed by law</u>. _____
3. Selling alcohol to minors is <u>unlawful</u>. _____
4. My <u>coworkers</u> generally agree with me. _____
5. She was <u>in jail</u> for six months. _____
6. Computer hacking is not considered to be a minor <u>crime</u>. _____
7. The student was severely <u>penalized</u> for cheating. _____
8. You can't kill someone and <u>not be punished for</u> it. _____
9. It's <u>shocking</u> that Draper could trick the phone company with a toy. _____
10. It's a <u>basic</u> fact of life: if you break the law, you might go to jail. _____

Vocabulary Builder ▲

Read the definitions of what these color words sometimes mean.
Can you guess the meaning of the underlined expressions?

black = excluded; illegal   **gray** = unclear
red = anger; danger   **white** = pale; afraid

1. You can get it for one-third the regular price <u>on the black market</u>.
2. I can't decide if it's a crime or not—it's <u>a real gray area</u>.
3. I had waited in line for hours. When I heard that the tickets were sold out, I <u>saw red</u>.
4. She said she'd seen a ghost. She was shaking and <u>as white as a sheet</u>.
5. Before the typhoon hit, the city issued <u>a red alert</u>.
6. I'd rather not invite him to our family reunion. He's <u>the black sheep of the family</u>.

▶ **Ask & Answer**

Whose opinion do you agree with in C on page 78? Think of a famous crime. Did the punishment fit the crime? Why or why not?

2 LISTENING
The story of DB Cooper

A Imagine that you're taking a museum tour using a headset to learn about criminal DB Cooper. Below are five exhibits that you're going to see as you listen to the tour. What crime do you think DB Cooper committed?

a sketch of DB Cooper   a handwritten note   a twenty-dollar bill
a photo of a Boeing 727   some FBI documents

B Now listen to the audio tour about DB Cooper and his crime. Put the following actions in the order in which they happened. (CD Tracks 22 & 23)

___ DB Cooper left the plane.
___ The passengers left the plane.
___ The plane departed for Seattle.
___ The plane departed for Mexico.
___ The FBI launched a search.
___ DB Cooper gave someone a note.
___ Some money was found.
_1_ DB Cooper boarded the plane.

C Listen again. Take notes on details about each exhibit that were important to investigators trying to solve the crime in the chart. (CD Track 24)

1: sketch	
2: photo of airplane	
3: handwritten note	
4: FBI documents	
5: twenty-dollar bill	

D Pair work. Compare your chart with a partner. Summarize what DB Cooper did. Then discuss the following questions.

1. Some people think DB Cooper is a kind of hero. What would make people think that?
2. Do you think he is a hero? Why or why not?

▶ **Ask & Answer**

What is one thing you would try to do if you thought you could get away with it?

3 LANGUAGE FOCUS

The past perfect

A Pair work. Read about these situations. Notice the words in blue. How is each situation different? In the second situation, why is the past perfect *(had jumped)* being used?

I saw someone breaking into my neighbor's home and called the police immediately. When the police arrived, the burglar jumped out the window, but they got a good look at him. I'm sure they'll catch him soon.

I saw someone breaking into my neighbor's home and called the police immediately. Unfortunately, by the tim the police arrived, the burglar had already jumped out the window. I'm not sure if they'll ever catch him.

B Read about a group of criminals called the Dinnertime Gang. Complete each sentence with the simple past or past perfect form of the verb in parentheses.

The Dinnertime Gang was one of the most successful crime gangs of all time. It's estimated they stole $70 million from over 3,000 homes. This sophisticated band of thieves stole high-priced jewels from their victims. Their crimes often occurred while their victims were at home, usually when they were having dinner.

The gang typically _____ (1. break into) wealthy homes after the residents _____ (2. turn off) their security alarms. Once inside, they worked quickly and quietly. People often realized they _____ (3. be robbed) days later when they _____ (4. go) to put on their jewelry and couldn't find it. Of course, by the time the police _____ (5. arrived) the criminals _____ already _____ (6. get away).

In one particular case, the gang pulled off a daring robbery. They knew that their victim _____ (7. receive) an expensive ring from her husband the month before. She only removed her ring when she went for a swim. On the evening of the theft, one gang member hid in the bushes. Once the woman _____ (8. leave) her bedroom to go to the pool, he _____ (9. climb) into the window and stole the ring. The gang later sold it for $350,000.

C Use the past perfect form of the verbs in the box to complete the e-mail message below.

~~be~~	freeze	not check in	see	travel
left	go	be pickpocketed	be stolen	

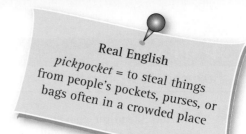

IN

Reply Forward Delete New Get Mail Trash

You have new mail!

Subj: back from my trip
From: Andre1027
To: mcrx1123

Hey Marco!
Well, my trip was terrible from start to finish. My flight from Montreal was scheduled for 7:00, but there **1.** ___had been___ a big storm earlier that morning, so the flight was delayed. I arrived at my destination three hours late, but my suitcase didn't. The baggage handlers **2.** _____ it at the Montreal airport accidentally.

Upon arrival at my destination, I learned that there was no bus service into the city. The bus drivers **3.** _____ on strike the day before. I took a taxi instead. It was expensive.

When I tried to check into my hotel, my credit card was declined. When I called the credit card company, they told me they **4.** _____ my card because they **5.** _____ never _____ an international charge on it before. An hour passed and I still **6.** _____ yet. At last, I was able to complete the process.

After checking in, I went for a walk on the beach. When I got back, I realized I **7.** _____. My wallet **8.** _____.

Before this trip, I **9.** _____ never _____ alone. I don't think I'll do it again anytime soon! Let me know when you're free to travel.

Andre

D Pair work. Think about a time when something bad happened to you because of a series of unfortunate events. Tell your partner about the experience.

- Your plane/bus/subway was delayed.

- Something important was lost.

- You had trouble buying something or using your credit card.

- Something was stolen from you.

- Your idea: _____

> One time, my taxi driver got lost. When we got to the airport, my plane had already taken off, so I had to . . .

A Pair work. Read the conversation between friends discussing a mistake on their bill at a restaurant. Tell your partner what you would do and why.

> **Ruth:** Let's see . . . the total is less than I thought it would be.
> Oh, I see why . . . The waiter forgot to write down our desserts.
>
> **Lori:** Really? Great! Free food!
>
> **Ruth:** Well, we should probably point out the mistake to the waiter.
>
> **Lori:** Why should we pay for his mistake? It seems to me that we only need to pay what the bill says. Look at it this way—I'm sure they sometimes overcharge people too. It all balances out in the end.
>
> **Keisha:** I wouldn't feel right about that. Don't you think we ought to say something? If we don't then the waiter might get into trouble.
>
> **Jessica:** Let's just tell the waiter, and have him change the bill.
>
> **Ruth:** I agree. If we were to walk out without paying for our desserts, it wouldn't be right.

B Write each example from the conversation under the appropriate heading.

Suggesting a course of action	Expressing a point of view gently	Considering consequences
We should probably . . .	It seems to me . . .	If we . . . then . . .
_____	_____	_____
_____	_____	_____

C Pair work. Role-play these situations. Talk about three possible things to do for each with your partner, and try to agree on a course of action.

1. You and your partner are at a store when you see an elderly woman putting some over-the-counter medicine into her shopping bag.

2. You and your partner work at a clothing store. A coworker wants a new dress to wear to a wedding but she can't afford one. She is planning to "borrow" a dress from the store, wear it to the wedding, and secretly return it to the store the next day.

D Pair work. Follow the steps below.

1. Think about a real-life situation in which you are not sure about the right thing to do.
2. Tell your partner the situation.
3. Discuss possible ways you could handle the situation.
4. Then tell your partner what you did and why.

E Group work. Work with another pair. Take turns presenting your situations.

They say "crime doesn't pay," but honesty might. There's a $5 million reward for helping the FBI solve the United States' largest art theft—The Gardner Museum Heist. The theft occurred in 1990 in Boston, MA, when two men dressed as police officers stole paintings worth $300 million USD.

Does Crime Pay?

| *Lesson B* | All kinds of criminals |

1 GET READY TO READ

A serious offense

 Have you ever witnessed a crime? What kind? What happened?

A Pair work. Read the information below each of the newspaper photos. Pay attention to the words in blue.

THE DAILY NEWS

4 April

The 20-year-old daughter of publishing executive Carson Randolph was **kidnapped** from her home in the early hours of Friday morning. Police believe that she was **abducted** as she left home for school. Her **kidnappers** have demanded . . .

At approximately 2:00 A.M. on Monday afternoon, an unknown white male held up the Bank of the East on Willshire Street. Witnesses say that the man approached the bank teller, took out a gun, and said, "This is a **robbery**. Give me your money and no one gets hurt." Anyone with information . . .

Star soccer player Ryan Neville was arrested for **disorderly conduct** after he was involved in a drunken fight in a local nightclub. Neville's teammates have all expressed surprise at his arrest. "Ryan's a serious athlete and a good guy. He's not a **troublemaker**," said Neville's coach. Neville is facing a punishment of . . .

B Complete the chart below with words from A.
Then describe each crime to a partner using your own words.

Crime	Verb	Criminal
kidnapping / abduction	<u>kidnap</u> / _____	_____ / abductor
_____	rob / _____	robber
_____	create a disturbance / cause trouble	_____

C Group work. What other crimes can you add to the chart in B? Share your ideas with the class.

▶ **Ask & *Answer***

Are any of these crimes a problem where you live? Why do you think people commit these kinds of crimes? What kind of punishment should they receive?

2 READING

Silly criminals, crazy crimes

A Skim the three articles on pages 84–85 and match each headline with the correct article. Write the article number next to the headline.

Men Arrested for Abducting Billionaire _____
Restaurant Diners Are Entertained _____
Towns Are Boring Once Again _____

B Read each of the articles and then complete the chart.

	Article 1	Article 2	Article 3
What crime was committed?			
Was/Were the criminal(s) arrested?	☐ yes ☐ no	☐ yes ☐ no	☐ yes ☐ no

1

A 25-year-old man has been arrested and charged with disorderly conduct for dressing up in a gorilla suit, jumping out of the bushes, and scaring local hikers in the southeastern region of Austria.

Though police had received several phone calls about gorilla sightings in the area, they ignored the reports at first. After repeated complaints, however, a surveillance* team, armed with guns and guard dogs, was set up, and authorities eventually captured the gorilla-suited prankster.

Why did he do it? The man explained that he had terrorized hikers because life in many of the little towns in the area seemed quite boring. "I just wanted to give people something to talk about," he explained.

The man was held for a day and later released after he apologized and handed in his gorilla suit.

surveillance: watching someone closely to see if they are involved in a criminal activity, usually by the police

2

Diners at a seafood restaurant about 140 kilometers south of Sydney, Australia, got an unexpected surprise last weekend when three armed robbers, all wearing heavy ski masks, attempted to enter the establishment to hold up the people inside. Scary stuff but fortunately for the diners, the thieves couldn't figur out *how* to get in the front door. For over a minute, the three men pushed and pulled at the clear-glass door tr to enter the restaurant while the shocked but amused diners looked on. What the unlucky trio hadn't noticed that the sign on the unlocked door read "slide." The g struggled for several minutes, and then finally gave up ran away.

Though the would-be thieves haven't been captured yet, police have identified a car that they be was used in the robbery attempt, and law enforceme officials have promised to conduct a thorough investi

C What makes the articles surprising or funny? Complete the sentences below.

Article 1: The man had dressed up _____.
He did this because _____.

Article 2: The criminals couldn't get in the restaurant because _____.

Article 3: Rose found out about Edward Lambert because _____.
Lambert's kidnappers were arrested when _____.

D Pair work. Rank the crimes in the articles from 1 (most serious) to 3 (least serious).
Compare your answers with a partner.

_____ Men Arrested for Abducting Billionaire.
_____ Restaurant Diners Are Entertained.
_____ Towns Are Boring Once Again.

Guessing meaning from context

E Pair work. The words and phrases below are from the articles. Categorize them in the chart and then work with a partner to write a simple definition for each one on another sheet of paper.

Use the words on either side of an unknown word to help guess its meaning.

Article 1:	~~capture~~	charge	~~terrorize~~	prankster
Article 2:	law enforcement officials	conduct an investigation		
Article 3:	mastermind	accomplice	apprehend	

Words describing police and what they do	Words describing criminals and what they do
capture	terrorize

3

Renaldo Rose, a 24-year-old former Marine, and three other men have been arrested for kidnapping business executive Edward Lampert, one of the richest men in the United States.

Rose, the group's mastermind, came up with a plan to kidnap Lampert after doing an Internet search for "wealthy businessmen in the Connecticut* area," and carefully researching Lampert's life. Rose then recruited and trained three accomplices to work with him. Soon after, the four men abducted Lampert at gunpoint from the office parking lot where he worked and took him to a hotel.

After holding him for almost thirty hours, Lampert's abductors offered to let him buy his freedom back. In turn, the businessman promised to give them $40,000 in cash in exchange for his release.

After receiving the cash, Rose and his accomplices dropped Lampert off near a local police station—which Lampert immediately visited. Within days, Rose and his partners were arrested. Thanks to great detective work by the police? Not quite. Turns out that one of Rose's partners had used Lampert's stolen credit card to have a pizza delivered, so they were easily apprehended by police!

*Connecticut: a state in the northeastern part of the U.S. near New York

▶ **Ask & Answer**

In your opinion, which of the crimes in the reading was the strangest? Why?
Do you know of any stories like the ones in the reading? What happened?

A Read this insurance company report. Notice where the past perfect is used and what kind of information has been included

Sunway Travelers' Insurance Report of loss or theft

Name: Brenda Coleman
Items lost/stolen: laptop computer

Date of incident: April 12
Brand: Lemon

Location: airport
Value: $2400

Describe the circumstances of the loss/theft:

My computer was stolen when I was checking in for a flight at the airport. I had gotten my boarding pass, and I was waiting in line for the security check. An old man in front of me had several large bags and he put them in the X-ray machine. I had just put my laptop on the table to be checked when the security guards asked the old man to empty his pockets. He dropped a lot of coins and keys all over the floor, so I helped him to pick them up. When I looked up, my laptop had disappeared. I told the guards and then they checked the area, but there was no trace of my computer. One of the guards told me that she had heard about two similar thefts in the past month.

B Pair work. Have you or someone you know ever had something stolen? Tell your partner how it happened.

C Write a narrative paragraph that you could use for an insurance report. Focus on providing only relevant information about sequences of events as they occurred. Use one of the situations below, or create your own.

Sunway Travelers' Insurance Report of loss or theft

Name:
Items lost/stolen:

Date of incident:
Brand:

Location:
Value:

Describe the circumstances of the loss/theft:

D Pair work. Read your partner's report. Ask questions about events that aren't described clearly enough.

Activity 1: What would you do?

Pair work. Read the situations below and decide what you would do in each one. Then explain your ideas to a partner. If your partner's opinion is different from yours, try to get him or her to agree with you.

1. You have a ten-page term paper to write for a class you're taking. You know a web site where you can buy term papers, and you are thinking of getting one and turning it in as your own. You can probably get away with doing this, but if you get caught, you could get an F in the class. Would you buy the term paper?

2. You're walking down the street when a frightened young woman carrying a small bag runs past you and hides in a doorway. Moments later, two men who say that they are undercover police approach you and ask if you've seen the woman. Would you tell them where she went?

3. You're trying to sell your bike when you notice that one of the tires is getting flat. The buyer hasn't noticed, though, and is willing to give you the price you're asking for the bike. Would you tell him or her about the tire?

4. While you're taking a test, the school fire alarm rings. It turns out that there was no fire and that someone had pulled the alarm as a joke. Later, you hear two of your classmates laughing about their prank. Would you report them?

Activity 2: You be the judge

A Pair work. Choose one of the articles on pages 84–85, and role-play the situation below.

> **Student A:** Take the role of one of the criminals from the articles you chose. Using your own words and ideas, explain why you committed the crime. Then try to convince the judge not to give you a serious punishment.

> **Possible Punishments**
>
> *I sentence you to 1 month / 10 years / life in prison.*
> *I'm going to fine you $500 / $2000 / $7000.*
> *You must do 10 / 100 / 500 hours of community service.*

> **Student B:** You are the judge. Listen to Student A, and ask him or her questions. Decide what type of punishment is suitable for the crime committed based on your partner's answers.

B Pair work. Switch roles. Choose a different article and repeat A.

 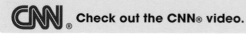

CNN ® **Check out the CNN® video.** **Practice your English online at** elt.heinle.com/worldpass

Unit 7: Does Crime Pay?

A Look at the meanings of colors in the box, and review the other meanings on page 79. Are the meanings similar or different in your language? Match the expressions with the sentences.

> pink = healthy, happy   yellow = fearful, cowardly   white = innocent
> green = jealous   blue = sad or dreamy   red = angry, debt

a. tickled pink   c. see red   e. a white lie   g. green with envy
b. in the red   d. yellow-bellied   f. blacklisted   h. feeling blue

1. Our boss was furious when she found out the report was late. ____
2. When Liza saw her sister's new car, she really wanted a car just like that. ____
3. Employers refused to give jobs to any members of that political party. ____
4. That criminal is hardly a brave man—he only attacks weak, elderly people. ____
5. The company I work for is always spending more money than it earns. ____
6. I was really homesick and depressed for the first few weeks after I moved to Australia. ____
7. I told my friend her new hairstyle looks cute, but actually, I think it looks kind of funny. ____
8. My grandmother was thrilled that I sent her a big bouquet of flowers for her birthday. ____

B Use your dictionary to help you write the name of the crime in the correct blank.

> robbery   murder   arson   shoplifting
> mugging   vandalism   speeding   burglary

1. Three teenagers broke all of the windows in the new high school building. _____
2. The police stopped a man who was driving 90 miles per hour through the main street downtown.

   _____
3. The salesclerk saw a girl putting CDs in her backpack without paying for them. _____
4. Someone started a fire in the office on the weekend when no one was there. _____
5. The woman was attacked as she was walking through the park at night and her purse was stolen.

   _____
6. I read in the newspaper about a man who killed his business partner in an argument about money.

   _____
7. Thieves in masks walked into the Capitol Bank and made the tellers give them all the cash in the drawer.

   _____
8. While she was on vacation, someone climbed in through the window and stole all her jewelry.

   _____

Watch out! incident and accident
Don't confuse these similar words for happenings. *Incident* is a neutral word for any kind of event. An *accident* is a sudden, negative, and unintentional event.

Expansion Pages

Incorrect: *I went to a party last night, but I was very boring.*

Correct: *I went to a party last night, but I was very <u>bored</u>.*

C Match these word combinations with their meaning.

> **Word combinations with *law***
>
> | | |
> |---|---|
> | 1. against the law ___ | a. commit a crime |
> | 2. obey the law ___ | b. illegal |
> | 3. break the law ___ | c. be made into a new law |
> | 4. enforce the law ___ | d. make people follow the law |
> | 5. become law ___ | e. do the right thing |
> | 6. by law ___ | f. according to the law |

D Use the correct form of the word combinations from **C** to complete the sentences.

1. In some countries, it's _____ law to hit a child for any reason.
2. In our city, you are required _____ law to wear your seat belt while driving.
3. The job of a police officer is to _____ law and protect citizens from danger.
4. The new regulations to control pollution of our country's rivers _____ law last year.
5. I try to always _____ law and keep to the speed limit on the highway.
6. That company _____ law by paying its workers less than the minimum wage.

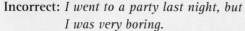

> A **criminal** is a person who has committed a crime: *Smith is one of the most dangerous criminals in our country.*
>
> **Crook** is an informal expression for a criminal or dishonest person: *Don't buy a used car from Jackson's Autos—that guy is a real crook!*
>
> A **thief** steals things: *The thief grabbed my purse from the restaurant table.*
>
> **Offender** is a legal term for someone who has committed a crime: *The court requires some offenders to do community service instead of a prison sentence.*

UNIT

8 Big Spender

Lesson A | Are you a savvy saver?

1 VOCABULARY FOCUS

What do you spend your money on?

 Which of the following do you usually spend your money on? Circle the words.

books / magazines   rent   movies   music
social life   clothing   trip   transportation
food   the gym   other: _____

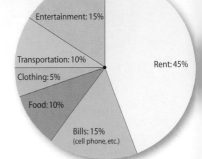

Entertainment: 15%
Transportation: 10%
Clothing: 5%
Food: 10%
Bills: 15% (cell phone, etc.)
Rent: 45%

A Pair work. Look at the pie chart of one person's spending habits.
Then draw your own chart on a separate piece of paper. Compare it with a partner.

B Read how these people answer the question, "What do you spend
your money on?" Pay attention to the words in blue.

Nikki, 25

That's an easy question! I love shopping and taking trips. I work in computer
programming . . . the hours are long and I believe in rewarding myself with something
nice as often as I can. For example, I go abroad at least twice a year. Saving money isn't
really a priority for me right now. Maybe I'll settle down in a few years.
Goal: Find a new job with a better salary and benefits (like health insurance and more
days off).

Most of my pay goes toward my house. I make good money, but I don't lead an
extravagant lifestyle, by any means. I don't drive a sports car or wear expensive clothes.
Once in a while, I like to splurge on a bottle of fine wine or an expensive dinner. But I
really have to budget carefully to make ends meet.
Goal: Invest more in the stock market. Put away money for retirement.

Vincenzo, 34

I live paycheck to paycheck and have to watch how I spend my money. It usually goes
toward sensible things, like groceries, gas, and my kids' education. Being a single mom is
rough! I can't squander money on silly things like electronic toys and fancy clothes I don't
really need. Still, sticking to a budget can be tough . . . everything costs so much money.
Goal: Get out of debt and then save some money.

Maria, 40

Takeshi, 27

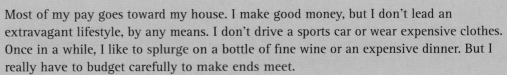

I inherited a lot of money from my grandparents and have been enjoying an easy life
for a while. My father says I can't sustain my expensive lifestyle forever—someday the
money will run out. I'm starting to think he's right. I've maxed out two of my credit
cards on things like vacations, cars, and expensive restaurants.
Goal: Get a job, get my finances in order, and pay off my credit cards!

C Pair work. Look at the words and phrases in blue in B. Which ones describe behavior about money? Write them in the correct column in the chart below.

Responsible behavior	Irresponsible behavior

▶ Ask & Answer
Are you able to stick to a budget and save money? What is your top priority in terms of money right now?

≫≫ Vocabulary Builder ▲▲

A. What is the meaning of *over* and *under* in the sentences below?

That dog is fat because his owner <u>overfeeds</u> him.   Daniel is so lazy. He's a total <u>underachiever</u>.

B. Complete the sentences below by combining *over* or *under* with a word in the box.

> charged   paid   estimated   priced   booked

1. People in my company tend to work long hours for little money. They're _____ but they still love their work.
2. That desk is ridiculously _____. We can find a cheaper one elsewhere.
3. The project was only supposed to last a day, but we worked for a week to finish it. We really _____ the amount of time it would take.
4. I think the waiter _____ us for our meal. My dinner was $15, but he's listed it on the bill as $25.
5. There are only one hundred seats on the plane, but the airline _____ it and sold 115.

2 LISTENING
We need a plan.

> Carrie and Joel are a young married couple who are meeting with Mr. Young, a financial advisor. Why do you think they are meeting with him?

A Listen and then complete the sentence. (CD Tracks 25 & 26)

Carrie and Joel are meeting with Mr. Young because

_____.

B Listen again. What suggestions does Mr. Young make? Take notes. Then mark how Joel and Carrie feel about his suggestions. (CD Track 27)

	the car	magazines / cable TV	entertainment
Mr. Young			
Carrie and Joel	☐ very positive ☐ less positive	☐ very positive ☐ less positive	☐ very positive ☐ less positive

C Pair work. Discuss the following questions.

1. What other ways can Carrie and Joel cut back on their expenses?
2. What do you think they will talk about after they leave Mr. Young's office?

▶ **Ask & Answer**

What do you spend money on each day? What could you cut back on? If you did that, how much money would you save in a week? A year? Ten years?

3 LANGUAGE FOCUS

Gerunds and infinitives

A Read the article about identity theft. Pay attention to the phrases in blue. Does each phrase contain a gerund or an infinitive? Underline the infinitives and circle the gerunds.

Identity theft is a big problem. It happens when a thief steals another person's personal information. The thief then pretends to be that person and illegally opens up bank accounts, borrows money, and runs up credit card bills until the money runs out. Identity theft is responsible for ruining the credit records of countless individuals.

Police say that some thieves rely on stealing information from online sites. Other thieves resort to digging through victims' garbage to locate credit card numbers and other information. Most identity thieves are not caught.

While many businesses work on improving security protection on their web sites, the problem of identity theft keeps growing. Peter Shaw is a victim of identity theft. Someone stole his credit card number when he decided to buy something online. The thief ran up bills in excess of $200,000 in Peter's name. Peter hopes to clear his name, but it is proving difficult. "Every time I finish solving one problem, another one pops up," says Peter.

Gerunds
A gerund is the *–ing* form of a verb that functions like a noun. A gerund can be the subject, the direct object, or the object of a preposition: • **Sticking** to a budget can be difficult.   • I like **spending** some money on myself once in a while.   • Adam dreams of **winning** the lottery someday.

Infinitives
An infinitive is *to* + the base form of a verb. An infinitive is often used as an object: • Gloria wants **to borrow** some money.

Large companies have tended to move slowly to chase after identity thieves, but that is changing as they lose billions of dollars in revenue and people avoid shopping online.

Peter is tired of writing letters and is fed up with making phone calls to clear his credit record. He has spent over 30 hours engaged in doing just that and he still isn't finished. "I refuse to buy anything online now. I don't enjoy doing it anymore," says Peter. "And I can't help worrying. I'm nervous about having my identity stolen again."

B Complete the chart with verbs from **A** that fit each pattern.

Verbs followed by gerunds	Verbs followed by infinitive
keeps growing	pretends to be
Verbs + preposition + gerund	**_Be_ + adjective + preposition + gerund**
rely on stealing	is responsible for ruining

C Read through the quiz below and complete each statement or question with the gerund or infinitive form of the verb in parentheses. Then take the quiz.

Are you a big spender or a savvy saver?

Circle the answer that best describes you.

1. In general, which statement best describes you?
   a. I'm **good at** (manage) _____ my finances and (stick) _____ to a budget.
   b. I'm **trying** (get) _____ my finances in order, and **hope** (save) _____ some money in the future.
   c. I don't really like to **think about** (budget) _____. I like (let) _____ others handle money issues for me.

2. How much of your income or allowance do you save each month?
   a. I **tend** (save) _____ at least 40–50% of it.
   b. I often **manage** (put away) _____ 10–20%.
   c. (Save) _____ money isn't really a priority for me right now.

3. Which statement best describes your use of credit cards?
   a. I don't have a card, or I **avoid** (use) _____ it unless I have to.
   b. I owe some money on my card(s), but not much.
   c. I'm **guilty of** (splurge) _____ quite often, and I've maxed out at least one card.

4. How do you **feel about** (lend) _____ money to others?
   a. I'm **nervous about** (do) _____ it, and normally, I **refuse** (lend) _____ money to others.
   b. I might do it if I really trusted the person.
   c. I **don't mind** (lend) _____ money to others.

5. You've just inherited some money. Which statement describes your plans?
   a. I **plan on** (invest) _____ the money or putting it away for retirement.
   b. I **intend** (save) _____ some of the money, but will probably use most of it to pay bills.
   c. I'm going to **quit** (work) _____ or (go) _____ to school and have some fun!

If your answers were:
Mostly As - You're a savvy saver. You're really smart with your money!
Mostly Bs - You're a balanced spender. Sometimes you splurge, sometimes you save.
Mostly Cs - You're a big spender. You'd better learn to watch your budget!

D Pair work. Interview your partner using the quiz above. Decide if your partner is more of a big spender or a savvy saver. Explain your decision to your partner.

E Pair work. A friend comes to you and is in debt. What advice would you give him or her? Take turns playing the part of the friend. Use gerunds and infinitives in your answers.

> You should never resort to borrowing money to pay off your debts.

> It's important to be careful about tracking your expenses.

> You should probably avoid using credit cards to make purchases.

> You should first stop spending money without a plan.

A Pair work. Match these sayings about money with their meanings.
Do you have any similar sayings in your language?

1. Money doesn't grow on trees. ___
2. We all need to save for a rainy day. ___
3. Money is no object. ___
4. Don't throw good money after bad. ___
5. Put your money where your mouth is. ___

a. Stop spending money on something that doesn't work.
b. Money is not easy to get.
c. It doesn't matter how much something costs.
d. Don't spend all your money—you may need it in case of problems.
e. If you really believe in something, you should be willing to spend money on it.

B Mina, a university student, is hoping to travel in Europe next summer, but she's on a tight budget. Read her friends' suggestions, noting the expressions in blue. Check (✓) the two best suggestions. Discuss your answers with a partner.

Making suggestions
1. Why don't you rent a car? Then you won't have to buy train tickets. ___
2. How about getting an international student card? It gives lots of discounts. ___
3. Have you thought about getting a job in Europe? You could make some money that way. ___
4. Have you considered going during winter instead? Prices are lower then. ___
5. What if you went to just one country? You'd save a lot of money on transportation. ___
6. Maybe you should check out travel web sites. They have some great deals. ___
7. You could camp somewhere instead of staying in hotels. That's a lot cheaper. ___

C Group work. Work in groups of three to role-play these situations. Student A has the problem, and Students B and C make as many suggestions as possible. Switch roles for each situation.

1. The books and other things I need for my classes are so expensive! I don't know how I can pay for them.
2. I like to go out with my friends and have fun, but my work schedule is so hectic I don't have time!
3. I'm really stressed right now. I really need to take a vacation and relax.
4. My friend always borrows my things, but she hardly ever returns them, and when she does, they're usually damaged!

D Class work. Take turns presenting your role plays to the class. As you listen to your classmates, write down all the ideas that you might try.

E Pair work. Tell a partner the three most useful tips you heard.

Big Spender

Lesson B | The global economy

1 GET READY TO READ

On the move

Have you ever lived in another country?
Where did you live? Why did you live there?

A Pair work. Read the profiles below. Pay attention to the words in blue. Complete the chart with a partner.

	Where from?	Lives where now?	Why moved?
Oleg			
Miranda's father			
Kazu			

A lot of things were changing in the Ukraine in the early '90s. The economy wasn't doing well. There was a lot of unemployment. In '93, my parents decided to emigrate. My dad's brother was already living here in California, and so this is where we moved. I was about ten at the time. When we arrived, we had to start from scratch—a new house, a new school for me, new jobs for my parents. I think moving was worth it, though. My family is very happy here.

My mom's from Argentina; my dad wasn't born here though, he's an immigrant actually. He's originally from Lebanon. When he moved to South America, he first lived in Brazil, and then later migrated here to Buenos Aires for a job. That's how he met my mom.

My family's from Tokyo, but we're pretty mobile because of my dad's work in the banking industry. We moved here to Singapore about a year ago. Before that we were in London for two years. There are a lot of things I like about moving around: seeing the world, meeting people from all over. These are opportunities most kids my age don't have. The downside is that it's kind of hard to make lasting friends.

B Match a word or phrase from A with its definition below. Write the word on the line.

1. leave one's country and move to another, usually permanently __emigrate__
2. operation of a country's money, businesses, and trade _____
3. chances to do something _____
4. begin again with nothing or very little _____
5. moved from one location to another _____
6. to be useful, helpful, or positive in some way _____
7. on the move, able to move quickly or easily _____
8. a person who comes to another country to live or work _____

▶ **Ask & Answer**

If you had the opportunity to work in another country, where would you like to go? Why?

2 READING
Money Makes the World Go Round

A Pair work. Read the two profiles on the right. Then read the phrases below. Check "A" for Arturo, "H" for Harish, or "B" for both. Then, with a partner, take turns talking about each man.

1. almost thirty years old ☐ A ☐ H ☐ B
2. sends money home ☐ A ☐ H ☐ B
3. works with computers ☐ A ☐ H ☐ B
4. went to graduate school ☐ A ☐ H ☐ B
5. lives in his ancestors' homeland ☐ A ☐ H ☐ B
6. is married ☐ A ☐ H ☐ B

> **Scanning for specific information**
>
> When you scan, you don't read every word. Instead, look over the reading passage quickly to find specific facts or ideas.

B Scan the Internet article on page 97 and match a statement below with the paragraph it summarizes. Write the number of the paragraph (1–6) next to the statement.

1. Why migrant workers are important to industrialized nations _____
2. How working abroad helps a person and his or her family _____
3. The number of people who are working abroad worldwide _____
4. How migrant workers are helping to improve their home countries _____
5. How Harish Singh feels about living in Canada _____
6. How and why immigration law is changing _____

C Read the article again. Complete these sentences with facts from the reading.

1. The number of people now living and working outside their country of birth is _____.

2. Migrant workers are important to many industrialized nations because _____.

3. The percentage of Indian nationals working in the U.S. is _____ and the amount of money they send home is _____.

4. The industrialized nations that have the largest number of migrant workers are _____.

5. Two important ways that immigration law is changing around the world are _____.

D Pair work. Summarize the main points of the reading in four to five sentences and tell your summary to a partner.

HARISH SINGH

Thirty-one-year-old Harish Singh works as a database programmer for a Vancouver biotechnology company. Born in Mumbai, India, Harish moved to Canada six years ago—fresh out of graduate school—when he was hired at the biotech company. The salary he earns in Canada is twice what he would've made back home, and the money helps his wife and children in India.

ARTURO GOMEZ

Twenty-nine-year-old Arturo Gomez, who is single, is a worker at an electronics factory south of Tokyo. Arturo's great-grandfather emigrated from Japan to Lima almost ninety years ago. Three generations later, Gomez has returned to the country of his ancestors' birth. The money that he sends back to Peru is helping his father buy a home and start a small family business.

Money Makes the World Go Round

1   Today, almost one out of every ten residents in many industrialized nations is from another country. The number of people living and working outside their home countries has more than doubled since the mid-1970s to almost 180 million today.

2   Arturo Gomez and Harish Singh are two of thousands of people who have traveled abroad in the last ten years in search of opportunity. Like Japan and Canada, countries in Europe, Australasia, and the Middle East are beginning to realize how important workers from abroad are to their economies. In some cases, migrant workers are providing industrialized nations with important skills that are lacking in the local population (especially in information and medical technology). In other cases, these mobile workers are willing to do certain jobs that many citizens won't do, such as janitorial and factory work.

3   By working abroad, Gomez and Singh are helping to improve their lives and those of their families. Money sent home can be used to buy a house, send someone to school, or start a small business. These are opportunities that families in some countries might not have otherwise.

4   The money that migrant workers are sending home is also having an impact on their countries of origin as well. The money functions as a kind of financial aid—helping to sustain, and sometimes improve, the economic well-being of the home country. In 2002, for example, Brazilian workers in Japan sent more money home than Brazil made by exporting coffee that year. Another statistic points out that a very small percentage (0.1%) of India's population lives and works in the U.S. However, these workers earn and send back almost *ten percent* of India's national income. In many places, money sent home by people like Harish Singh is helping to reduce poverty* in communities throughout the country.

5   The money that migrant workers are sending home is also influencing immigration law in countries worldwide in a couple of important ways. Industrialized nations that have the largest number of migrant workers (the first is the U.S., followed closely by Saudi Arabia, Germany, and Japan) are now making it easier for foreign workers to enter, and remain in, their countries. Another important effect is that many countries are now allowing dual citizenship—which was quite uncommon in the recent past, especially in developing nations. Now, a citizen of one country can live and work abroad as a citizen of another nation, and still send money back to his or her home country.

6   Back at home after work, Harish is getting ready to phone his parents in Mumbai. "Missing my family has been the hardest part of living in Canada," he says. "I mean, I love it here, but every so often, I do get homesick." He pauses. "But I know I made the right decision to move here. In the long run, I know that all I'm doing now will be worth it."

*poverty: the state of being very poor

▶ **Ask & Answer**
Do you know anyone who has moved far away from his or her family to make more money? Do you think you could do it? What would be the hardest part?

A Pair work. Discuss the meanings of these statements with your partner. Then complete the opinion survey below. Compare your answers.

Beliefs about money	Strongly agree	Agree	Disagree	Strongly disagree
1. Money makes the world go round.				
2. The love of money is the root of all evil.				
3. Money isn't everything.				
4. Waste not, want not.				
5. Anybody can get rich if they work hard enough.				

B Read the information in the box. Then, follow the steps and complete the outline below.

> **Argument paragraphs**
>
> When you write an argument paragraph, you want to persuade your readers to agree with your opinion. To do this, you give reasons for your opinion, and use examples to help readers understand these reasons.

Step 1. Choose one belief from the survey in A that you strongly agreed or disagreed with.
Step 2. Use the belief as the topic for an argument paragraph. Write a topic sentence that expresses your opinion about the statement.
Step 3. Support your opinion by giving three specific reasons with examples from your life.

Belief: _____

Topic sentence: _____

Reason 1: _____

Example 1: _____

Reason 2: _____

Example 2: _____

Reason 3: _____

Example 3: _____

C Write your argument paragraph on a separate piece of paper.

World Link

D Pair work. Read your partner's paragraph. Ask questions about anything that is unclear. Then make two polite suggestions for improving the paragraph.

What if you gave more details about . . . ?

I'm not clear on what you mean by . . .

> $6,000 for a wig? $9,500 a week on veterinary bills? $72,000 a month on flowers? Sound a little over your budget? Not if you're British pop star Elton John, who reportedly earned over £33 million ($62 million USD) in 2004 alone!
>
> Source: *Yahoo! News UK & Ireland*

Activity 1: Talk for a minute

A Read the questions below and think about possible answers.

1. What was the most extravagant restaurant, party, or social event that you've ever been to like?
2. Imagine that you could change lives for a day with a person of great wealth. Who would you change places with? Why?
3. What is something you're saving up for?
4. If you inherited a large sum of money, what is the first thing you'd spend it on? Why?
5. What is something you'd never do for money?
6. Have you ever splurged and bought something expensive that later you didn't use?
7. Do you agree or disagree with the saying, "Giving is better than receiving?"

B Group work. Get into a group of three people. Follow the directions below.

1. For this activity, you need a watch and seven small pieces of paper.
2. Number the pieces of paper from 1–7. Put the numbers face down.
3. One person chooses a number and finds the matching question in A.
4. The person answers the question. If he or she can talk for one minute *without stopping*, the person gets a point.
5. The speaker returns the paper and it's the next person's turn.
6. Continue until all questions have been answered once. The person with the most points wins.

Activity 2: The chance of a lifetime

A Group work. Get into a group of six. One pair should be the Investors. The other two pairs should be the Entrepreneurs. Read your information below and follow the directions.

The Investors	You and your partner are attorneys for a very wealthy family that invests in new businesses and helps young entrepreneurs get started. Every year, the family donates the equivalent of one million dollars to a worthy candidate. This year, the family is interested in investing money in people who want to start businesses abroad. Find out more about the Entrepreneurs by asking the questions below. Then add three or four questions of your own. • In which country have you decided to spend your two years? Why have you chosen this country? • What are you interested in doing with the money? What kind of business do you plan to start? • If you're awarded the money, how do you intend to spend it? Create a simple budget to describe your plans. • What difficulties do you think you'll face in your new country? How are you planning to overcome these?
The Entrepreneurs	You and your partner have decided to travel the world in search of opportunity. You are planning to leave your country, and spend two years abroad in _____ (name the country). In your opinion, this is the place where you will most likely be able to make money and be successful. Your goal is to convince the Investors that you are the best pair to give the money to. Discuss the questions below.

B Group work. The Investors question each pair of Entrepreneurs, and decide which pair gets the money.

  Check out the CNN® video. **Practice your English online at elt.heinle.com/worldpass**

Unit 8: Big Spender

Expansion Pages

A Look at the list of expenses and the household budget chart. Write the expenses in the correct categories. What are the three biggest categories in your own budget? Circle them.

Expenses

student loans	tuition	movies	mortgage payments	gasoline
electricity	hobbies	lunches at work	rent	groceries
clothing	bus tickets	shoes	water	

Household budget

1. Housing	
2. Utilities	
3. Food	
4. Apparel	
5. Transportation	
6. Education	
7. Entertainment	

B English has many informal expressions for attitudes toward money. Look at these terms and write each below the correct picture. Use your dictionary as necessary. Which words best describe you? Circle them.

> miser   spendthrift   shopaholic   big spender   tightwad   cheapskate   penny-pincher

1. _____

2. _____

C What do these cost expressions mean? Write *I* (inexpensive) or *E* (expensive) after each word or phrase.

1. costly _____
2. a bargain _____
3. reasonable _____

4. pricey _____
5. out of my price range _____
6. exorbitant _____

7. economical _____
8. a good value _____
9. a rip-off (informal) _____

I didn't know that!

In Europe, centuries ago, banks would give their best customers ceramic "borrower's tiles." These tiles had the customer's name and the name of the bank imprinted on them, similar to a credit card today. When a customer wanted to borrow more money, he would take his borrower's tile to the bank and show it to the teller. If the customer had already borrowed too much money, the teller took his tile and "broke" it.

D Use the word combinations in the box to complete the sentences.

Word combinations with *cost*	
pay the cost (of something)	high-cost/low-cost
the cost of (doing something)	rising cost
at no extra cost	cost of living

1. If you buy a new computer during our summer sale, we'll also give you a printer _____.
2. Because I have to work until midnight every night this week, my boss offered to _____ of my taxi home.
3. The city is going to build an area of _____ housing, to help poor families move out of the slums.
4. The _____ of oil is making gasoline more expensive every day.
5. Tokyo has a very high _____ due to the lack of affordable housing.
6. Many companies are building factories in other countries because _____ production is lower there.

In Other Words

Money is the general word for what you spend to buy things: *Can you lend me some money?*
Cash means coins and bills (not checks or credit cards): *That store only accepts cash.*
Change is the money you get back when you pay for something in a store: *I gave the clerk $10, and he gave me 80 cents in change.*
Currency is the money of a particular country: *I changed 100,000 yen into British currency at the bank.*

A **price** is the amount of money charged for something in a store or restaurant: *The prices at Gold's Department Store are really high.*
The **cost** is the amount of money you pay for an activity: *The cost of my vacation was less than $1000.*
You pay a **fee** to enter a place: *The entrance fee for the museum is reduced on Sundays.*
You pay a **charge** for a service, or to use something: *There is a $2 charge to send a fax from the hotel.*
You pay a **fare** to travel on a plane/bus/boat, etc.: *The subway fare in my city went up last month.*

Watch out!

borrow and lend
These verbs do NOT have the same meaning. When we *borrow* something, we receive it temporarily. When we *lend* something, we give it temporarily.

1 VOCABULARY FOCUS

Family issues

 When you hear the word "family," what words or images come to mind?

A Pair work. These two couples posted questions on an online bulletin board.
Work with a partner to match each headline with its posting. What is each couple's problem?

a. Too Young to Fit in _____   b. Trying to Find Common Ground _____

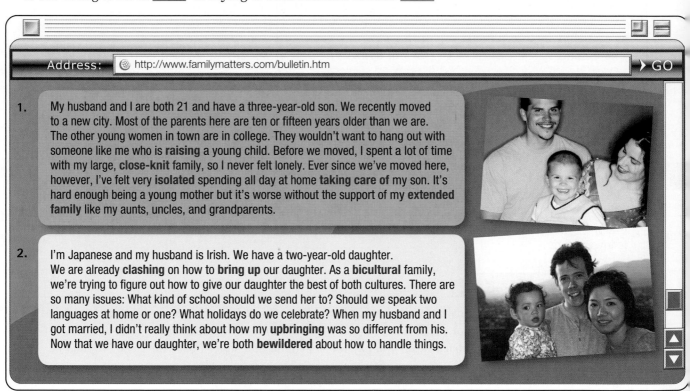

Address: http://www.familymatters.com/bulletin.htm ❭ GO

1. My husband and I are both 21 and have a three-year-old son. We recently moved to a new city. Most of the parents here are ten or fifteen years older than we are. The other young women in town are in college. They wouldn't want to hang out with someone like me who is **raising** a young child. Before we moved, I spent a lot of time with my large, **close-knit** family, so I never felt lonely. Ever since we've moved here, however, I've felt very **isolated** spending all day at home **taking care of** my son. It's hard enough being a young mother but it's worse without the support of my **extended family** like my aunts, uncles, and grandparents.

2. I'm Japanese and my husband is Irish. We have a two-year-old daughter. We are already **clashing** on how to **bring up** our daughter. As a **bicultural** family, we're trying to figure out how to give our daughter the best of both cultures. There are so many issues: What kind of school should we send her to? Should we speak two languages at home or one? What holidays do we celebrate? When my husband and I got married, I didn't really think about how my **upbringing** was so different from his. Now that we have our daughter, we're both **bewildered** about how to handle things.

B Pair work. Now read responses two people made to the postings in A. Match each response to the appropriate family. What advice would you give to each family?

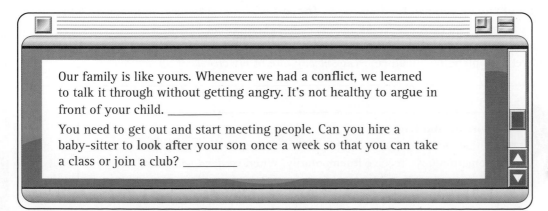

Our family is like yours. Whenever we had a **conflict**, we learned to talk it through without getting angry. It's not healthy to argue in front of your child. _____

You need to get out and start meeting people. Can you hire a baby-sitter to **look after** your son once a week so that you can take a class or join a club? _____

Real English
talk it through = discuss something thoroughly and calmly to reach a decision

C Pair work. Look at the expressions in blue in A and B and classify them.
With a partner, come up with a definition for each expression.

Words related to caring for children	Words that describe families	Words that describe disagreement	Words that describe feelings
raising			

Vocabulary Builder ▲

Read the definitions of these words that are used to describe families.
Then complete the sentences with the words below.

adoptive family = the family of a child who has been adopted
biological family = the family that you're born into
immediate family = family members that are closest to you (e.g., parents, children, brothers and sisters)
nuclear family = the traditional family unit of parents and children

1. I'm sorry, but hospital visitors are limited to ___immediate___ family members only.
2. Some people are worried about the breakdown of the traditional _____ family.
3. Tammy gave birth to Hudson. She and her husband are Hudson's _____ family.
4. My sister couldn't keep her son. He was raised by the Smith family. The Smiths are his _____ family.

2 LISTENING

Giorgio's ad

> Who takes care of the elderly in your community?

Real English
snap decision = decision made quickly, without much thought

A Listen to this radio report about Giorgio Angelozzi, an 80-year-old pensioner. Why did he become famous? Write your answer. (CD Tracks 28 & 29)

_____

B Listen and circle the correct answer to complete each statement. (CD Track 30)

1. Giorgio's immediate family includes one / two / three child(ren).
2. Giorgio had worked as a postman / professor / lawyer.
3. Giorgio's worst problem was that he was poor / lonely / sick.
4. Giorgio decided to move in with a family from the U.S. / Colombia / Italy.
5. The Riva family heard about him on TV / on the Internet / by word of mouth.
6. The family had no children / one child / two children.
7. The family wanted to adopt Giorgio because the father's parents had died / were living in another country, and the mother's parents were dead / were living in another country.
8. Giorgio chose this family because they were friendly and they loved cats / had a lot of money / all signed a letter to him.

▶ Ask & Answer

What do you think of Giorgio's personal ad?

Would you ever place or respond to an ad like Giorgio's?

A Read the sentences. Notice the words in blue.

> Relative clauses define or identify nouns (people, places, and things) or give additional information about them.
>> In Italy, there is an increasing number of older people who have no one to look after them.
>
> The relative pronouns *who, that,* or *which* are followed by a verb in a subject relative clause. That verb agrees with the noun that the clause is modifying.
>> Giorgio has a new family that *lives* in the north of Italy.
>> Giorgio has new grandchildren that *live* in the north of Italy.

B Read about the Park family. Then follow the steps below.

It's 5:00 A.M. and the alarm clock is going off in the Park family apartment. Jenny, who is the oldest of the three children, has to get up. She's just another junior high school student who has a big test today. But before she goes to school, she needs to go to an audition. The audition, which is far from her home, begins at 6:15 A.M. It's a tough schedule that takes a lot of drive and commitment.

The Park family used to live in a large apartment building that was located in the center of Seoul, Korea. They were a close-knit family. Two years ago, Mrs. Park moved with her three children to New York City. Mr. Park, who couldn't leave his job in Seoul, stayed behind. There's a reason for the separation. Jenny is an outstanding violinist and wanted to study with a famous teacher that lives in New York, Jack Goldman.

"At first, my parents clashed over the issue of separating the family," says Jenny. "But finally, my father agreed to it."

"It's hard to raise children in a foreign place. Sometimes I feel so isolated here," says Mrs. Park. "Our old life, which was more predictable, was easier." The sacrifice, however, is worth it, she says. "We couldn't pass up this opportunity to study with Mr. Goldman. Who knows . . . maybe someday my daughter will be famous."

1. Underline the subject relative clauses and circle the relative pronouns. What noun is being modified in each case?
2. Which relative pronouns are used to talk about people? Which ones are used to talk about things?

C Read about the different kinds of clauses. Notice the use of commas.
Which clauses in **B** are defining relative clauses? Which ones are nondefining?

Defining relative clauses	Nondefining relative clauses

A defining relative clause cannot be omitted because it is needed to make the meaning of the sentence clear:
   I saw the man who robbed the store.
	A nondefining relative clause can be omitted because it adds extra information. The meaning of the sentence is clear without it:
	   My father, who is 45, works downtown.

D Read these sentences about a person's family and underline the relative clauses.
Write "D" for defining and "N" for nondefining. Add commas where necessary.

1. __N__ I was brought up by an extended family. I grew up in the 1990s, which was a very happy time for me.

2. ____ I have two older brothers. The one who was born in 1980 lives in London. His name is Randy.

3. ____ My other brother is named Rafael. He runs a successful business which is located in our hometown.

4. ____ Here's a photo of my family. The woman who's standing in the back row is my sister.

5. ____ My mother who raised four children now looks after my grandparents. They live downstairs.

6. ____ My parents have been married for almost thirty years. We're planning a party for them on May 17 which is their anniversary.

7. ____ The party that is being planned will go all night. We've invited over 100 guests.

8. ____ My parents who don't know about the party are going to be very surprised!

E Read about this famous family. Combine the sentences into one, using a subject relative clause.

1. Francis Ford Coppola suffered from polio as a boy. He grew up to be a famous Hollywood director and producer.
   <u>Francis Ford Coppola, who suffered from polio as a boy, grew up to be a famous Hollywood director and producer</u>.

2. Coppola directed *The Godfather*. It won many awards.
   _____
   _____

3. His daughter, Sophia, is also in the film industry. She directed the movie *Lost in Translation*.
   _____
   _____

4. Many years ago Coppola appeared in a Japanese commercial. The commercial influenced the plot of *Lost in Translation*.
   _____

5. Coppola's nephew is actor Nicolas Cage. Cage won an Oscar for his performance in *Leaving Las Vegas*.
   _____

6. In 2002, Lisa Presley and Nicolas Cage had a brief marriage. It ended in divorce.
   _____

F Group work. Think of a well-known person, place, or thing.
Describe it in two sentences. Can your partners guess it?

> I'm thinking of a rock group that comes from Ireland. They are very popular. The lead singer, who is politically active, goes by one name only.

> Is it U2?

4 SPEAKING

A lot of people think . . .

A   Read the conversation. Notice the expressions in blue.

Angela: Have you heard? Rob and Trish are getting a divorce. She called me last night.

Elise: Oh no! Really? That's too bad . . . and it's going to be awfully hard for their kids.

Angela: Yeah, **but on the other hand** it has to be really hard for them to hear their parents fighting all the time.

Elise: Well, **I don't think** couples should divorce if they have young kids. **It's obvious** that kids need both parents at home. Some parents only think of themselves.

Angela: I'm not so sure about that. **A lot of people think** that single parents can't raise healthy kids. **But in reality,** lots of kids grow up just fine with divorced parents. I bet you know some yourself.

Elise: **Still, you can't deny that** children do better when they live with both parents. Divorce is just too easy these days.

Angela: Getting a divorce doesn't mean the end of the family. Lots of divorced couples work out a better relationship afterwards, so they can be better parents, for the children's sake.

Elise: Maybe, **but** it would be better for everyone if they tried working out their relationship before they got a divorce.

B   Who do you think would agree with these ideas? Check (✓) the boxes.

	Angela	Elise
1. Parents who get divorced are acting selfishly.		
2. Single parents do a good job.		
3. Couples don't try hard enough to save their marriages.		
4. In a divorce, couples need to consider their children's needs		

C   Find expressions in the conversation in A to complete the chart.

Stating your case	Answering the other case / Rebutting
The fact of the matter is . . . It's clear that . . . You can't deny that . . . _____ _____	Some people say . . . / But . . . It may seem that . . . / But actually . . . _____ / But _____ . . . _____ . . . / But _____ . . .

D   Pair work. You and your partner pick one of these statements and choose opposite points of view. Take a minute to think of ideas you can use. Then discuss the topic, using expressions from the chart in C.

1. It seems to me that marrying someone from another culture brings a lot of problems / benefits.
2. It's a good / bad idea for kids to take supplementary lessons after school.
3. I think university students should / should not live with their parents.
4. I think it's OK / not OK for parents to discipline their children by hitting them.

Family Matters

Lesson B | Families past and present

1 GET READY TO READ

The changing family

 Think about families during your grandparents' generation, your parents' generation, and now yours. Have things changed for families over the years? In what ways?

A Read about four ways that the modern family is changing. Then look at the list of possible causes below and choose the one(s) that you think explain(s) each change.

The divorce rate is rising.

People are getting married later or not at all.

Fewer couples are having children.

Family members don't live near each other.

Possible causes:

It's easier to divorce than it was in the past.
The cost of living is higher these days.
People have jobs that force them to relocate.
Women have more options than they did in the past.

Both parents have to work.
People are more selfish.
Our lives are more hectic.
Other: _____

B Pair work. Combine two sentences from above using cause / effect words and phrases to share your opinion with a partner. Do you think all of the changes are negative?

>   effect   cause
> The divorce rate is rising *because* it's easier to divorce than it was in the past.
>   cause   effect
> It's easier to divorce than it was in the past; *therefore*, the divorce rate is rising.

Friends: Today's New Family

A Pair work. What makes a family different from other groups of people?
Compare your ideas with those of a partner.

B Read the title of the article on page 109. What do you think the article is about?
Write down your ideas on a piece of paper. Then read the article to see if you were right.

C Pair work. What does the author mean by "Friends: Today's New Family"? Discuss your ideas with your partner.

D Answer the questions with information from the reading.

1. Professor Kumar gives two reasons to explain why people are living outside of traditional families and moving in with friends. List them.
   _____

2. Why was life in Seattle tough for Javier and Juliana? List two reasons.
   _____

3. Why did Peter and Birgit think about moving back to Germany? List two reasons.
   _____

4. Javier, Juliana, Peter, Birgit, and their children now share a house together. What are two positive effects of this?
   _____

5. What is the main reason that Illeana, Liam, and Simone decided to move in together?
   _____

E Pair work. Compare your answers in D with your partner, using phrases for cause and effect.

> *People are living outside of traditional families because the divorce rate is rising.*

F Write the correct word or phrase from the reading on the lines below.

1. On line 16, another way to say *traditional* or *usual* is _____.
2. On line 26, another way to say *in the same situation as someone else* is _____.
3. On line 28, another way to say *making life very difficult* is _____.
4. On line 31, another way to say *to put all your money together for a common goal* is _____.
5. On line 44, another way to say *to rely on or ask for help from another* is _____.
6. On line 45, another way to say *to give someone help or support* is _____.

Reminder: Guessing meaning from context

Use the words on either side of an unknown word to help guess its meaning.

World Link

Immigrants to the U.S. are much more likely to live in traditional families than non-immigrants. In the year 2000, only 23% of all non-immigrant U.S. families were married couples with their own children, compared with 72% of the families that had immigrated to the U.S. after 1990.

Source: *U.S. Census Bureau*

Friends: Today's New Family

It's 7:30, and Javier Perez rushes into the kitchen and kisses his wife Juliana and their two-year-old son before quickly swallowing a glass of orange juice. A moment later, Javier and Juliana's friends Peter and Birgit come into the room with their three-year-old daughter. Peter puts the little girl at the kitchen
5   table while Birgit pours her a bowl of cereal.

"You guys want anything for breakfast?" asks Juliana.
"Not this morning, thanks. We're running late," replies Peter. "We'll pick something up on the way to work."
"See you tonight then."

10   What's happening here? To an outsider, it might appear that one family is visiting another. But, in fact, these are two unrelated families that have chosen to share one household together. Like a growing number of people today, their friends are their family.

When many people hear the word "family," they think of the nuclear or extended
15   model. However, while at least 40 to 50% of the world's population still belongs to a traditional family unit, many more people today are living outside conventional family relationships. According to Ajay Kumar, a professor of sociology at Whaterston University, there are several reasons for this. "Divorce rates all over the world are on the rise," notes Kumar. "Also, people are a lot more mobile these days—which often breaks
20   up the traditional family network."

Juliana and Javier Perez understand this all too well. "Julie and I moved to Seattle about a year after graduating from college and eventually married and had a son," recalls Javier, now 34. "But it was tough. Everything was so expensive and so we both had to work full time. Also, we had almost no help with the baby since my family is in Florida, and
25   Juliana's folks are in Maine. So when we needed help, we turned to our friends."

Peter and Birgit, whom Javier and Juliana had met after they moved to Seattle, were in the same boat. "Peter and I were struggling, too," says Birgit, who is originally from Frankfurt, Germany. "We couldn't afford a house of our own. Day-care costs were killing us. Consequently, we even considered moving back to Germany to be close to my family, though neither Peter nor I really wanted to do that."

30   When Peter and Birgit told Juliana and Javier that they were planning to move, Javier had an idea. "I thought, why not pool our resources, buy a place together, and create something that could benefit us all?" Four months later, the two families purchased and moved into a two-story house. "We each have our private space—the first floor has two bedrooms as does the second floor," explains Javier. "We share the living room, dining area, and the kitchen." And the results, so far, have been positive. "There's always someone around to lend a hand with the cooking and shopping," laughs Javier. "And
35   Peter and Birgit's daughter is like an older sister to my son."

Couples with children aren't the only ones changing the definition of family. Many people who are marrying at a later age or are choosing not to marry at all will often form long-term shared households with friends. Illeana Phillips is a 37-year-old sales associate who has shared a London flat with her friends Simone and Liam for the last three years. "We've been friends since college, and we all had jobs and places of our own," says Phillips. "But I think that each of us was kind of
40   lonely and bored living alone so we decided to get a place together." Illeana pauses. "Personally speaking, this situation works well for me because I might never get married and have a family of my own." A shared household provides the kind of financial and emotional support that is similar to that of a traditional family.

Illeana's housemate, Simone, sums it up this way, "Some say that blood is thicker than water—you know, that your family ties are the strongest—but for me, my friends are my family. They're the ones that you can always turn to for help and
45   encouragement. They'll stand by you for life."

▶ **Ask & Answer**

Do you think that people who are not related by blood or marriage can be like family? Are any of your friends like family to you?

Conclusion sentences

A Read this paragraph and underline the topic sentence. The conclusion
sentence is in blue. How is it related to the topic sentence?

For many young adults living alone in large cities, a close group of friends is their best support network. Writer Ethan Watters calls these groups "urban tribes," circles of friends that are important to young singles who live far from their families. These urban tribes help people deal with the problems of city life by providing companionship and practical help. If you're feeling lonely on Saturday night or need help finding a plumber, you can call on the members of your "tribe." They can also provide support in times of trouble—such as going grocery shopping for a friend who has a broken leg. In many respects, an urban tribe is like a second family.

B Underline the topic sentences in these paragraphs. Then add conclusion sentences.

1. When companies provide child-care facilities for their employees with young children, it's not only the workers who benefit. Employees who don't have to worry about their children during business hours can devote their full attention to the job. Furthermore, studies have found that employees lose less time from work due to children's illnesses when day care is provided on-site. And companies that offer child care have a strong advantage in attracting highly qualified employees. _____
_____

2. Many people mistakenly believe that a househusband has an easy life. When a father decides to leave his job and stay home to care for his children, he looks forward to teaching his kids and enjoying daily life with them. But he often isn't prepared for the downside. Many househusbands get tired of the isolation of spending their days without other adults for company. They miss their friendships with colleagues at the office. Worst of all is the lack of respect from people who ask questions such as, "But what do you *really* do all day?"_____
_____

C Complete the outline with your opinions.

Should elderly parents live with their children?   Yes   No
Reason 1: _____
Reason 2: _____
Reason 3: _____

D Write a paragraph using your outline from C. Be sure to include
examples and explanations, and a strong conclusion.

E Pair work. Exchange paragraphs with your partner.
Are there any ideas that you disagree with?

> *It may seem that people are selfish when they put
> their parents in a nursing home, but in fact . . .*

Activity 1: Class poll

A Class work. Read the polling question below and think about how you'd answer it.
Then take a class vote. Which response got the most votes and why?

> **Quick Poll**
>
> Imagine that your parents are elderly. They want to live alone, but they
> are slowing down and you are worried. What would you do?
>
> a) I'd suggest they move into a nursing home. _____
> b) I'd ask them to move into my home. _____
> c) I'd pay for them to have round-the-clock care from a nurse in their own home. _____

B On your own, come up with a polling question about the topic of family with three or
four possible answer choices. Choose from the ideas below or think of your own.

Topics to ask questions about:
- the best place to raise a family
- the most serious issue facing families today
- best age getting married, having kids
- living with parents after marriage
- your favorite relative

- biracial/bicultural families
- a man's or woman's role in the family
- best way to discipline children
- grown children living with their parents
- other: _____

C Class work. Ask your classmates your polling question. Keep track of the responses
you get. Also, ask people to give you a simple explanation for their answer choices.

D Pair work. Get together with a partner and explain the results of your poll.
Which response got the most votes? What are some reasons people gave
for their answers?

> *The question I asked was, What's the best place
> to raise a family? Answer B got the most votes.
> People who chose answer B think . . .*

Activity 2: What's your definition?

A Write a simple definition for each item below.
Add one of your own categories to the list.

What's your definition of . . .

1. a happy family? _____
2. a good father? _____
3. a true friend? _____
4. a good mother? _____
5. an ideal partner (spouse/boyfriend/girlfriend)? _____
6. a fun vacation? _____
7. the perfect date? _____
8. your idea: _____

B Pair work. Compare your definitions with a partner. Give examples from your own experience to explain your ideas.

 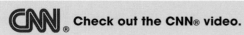 **Check out the CNN® video.**   **Practice your English online at elt.heinle.com/worldpass**

Unit 9: Family Matters

A Look back at the Vocabulary Focus on pages 102–103. Complete each row in the chart with the appropriate form of the word. Then use some of the words to complete the sentences below.

Verb	Adjective	Adjective	Noun
	adopted	adoptive	
extend			extension
	isolated	----	

1. Al has a large _____ family. He has about 20 aunts and over 50 cousins!
2. _____ parents love their children just as much as biological parents do.
3. I used to live in the country far from the nearest town, but I couldn't stand the _____. I was too lonely.
4. When Maria moved to Rome, she didn't know anyone. She felt very _____ until she met some friends at work.
5. I think Billy must be _____. He doesn't look anything like his brothers and sisters.

B Match the terms with their meanings.

1. A family name ___.
2. A family tree ___.
3. A family doctor ___.
4. A family man ___.
5. The family circle ___.
6. A family room ___.
7. A family reunion ___.

   a. is the group of people who are your close relatives
   b. is one who likes to be at home with his wife and children
   c. is one who treats patients of all ages
   d. is a diagram that shows all your relatives
   e. is a surname
   f. is a place where people watch TV and relax together
   g. is a big party with all your relatives

C Complete the sentences with a term from **B**.

1. I really enjoyed the family _____ because I got to see all of my cousins.
2. Since his son was born, Alex has become a real family _____. He never goes out with his friends anymore!
3. Kim and Park are very common family _____ in Korea.
4. My sister did a lot of research and drew our family _____, going back more than 200 years.
5. You really shouldn't talk about your brother's problems outside of our family _____.
6. I want to buy a new sofa for the family _____ because we spend so much time there.
7. I really prefer to see my family _____ rather than a specialist because she knows all of us and our problems so well.

Tricky English

Incorrect: *I fell in love with my wife the first time I sawed her.*

Correct: *I fell in love with my wife the first time I saw her.*

Expansion Pages

D Review the meaning of these words from "Friends: Today's New Family" on page 109. Then use the correct form of the word to complete the sentences.

> mobile (para 4)　　eventually (para 5)　　rush (para 1)　　network (para 4)
> struggle (para 6)　　pool (para 7)　　long-term (para 8)　　flat (para 8)

1. When we were teenagers, my brother and I _____ our money and bought a very cheap old used car.
2. I think living with friends is OK when you're young, but it's not a good _____ plan.
3. When Kim moved to London, she had a hard time finding a _____ because rents are so high.
4. The teacher gave us only three days to do the project, so we had to really _____ to finish it in time.
5. Luis is a single father, and he's really _____ to raise two kids while working full-time.
6. Many students build up a _____ of friends during their university years who will help them later in professional life.
7. In today's business world, companies are more _____, and many are increasingly sending their operations outside their home country.
8. I plan to attend medical school, study tropical diseases, and _____ work in a developing country.

E A number of everyday terms are different in American English and British English. Match the equivalent nouns.

> a. tick　　c. petrol　　e. torch　　g. lift　　i. cinema
> b. tap　　d. CV　　f. chemist's　　h. rubbish　　j. city centre

1. gasoline ___　　3. garbage ___　　5. drugstore ___　　7. faucet ___　　9. résumé ___
2. elevator ___　　4. flashlight ___　　6. checkmark ___　　8. downtown ___　　10. movie theater ___

In Other Words

Your **home** is the place where you live and feel comfortable. The word has a positive emotional feeling: *I was born in Korea, but Los Angeles is my home now.*
A **house** is a type of building: *I live in a small, two-bedroom house.*
Residence is a formal or legal term: *The governor's residence is a big, white mansion.*
A **household** is all the people who live together in one house: *There are three people in our household: my two roommates and me.*

If two people or groups **clash**, they fight or argue because of different views or beliefs: *The two political parties clashed over how to improve the nation's economy.*
Disagree is a more general term, meaning "have a different idea": *I disagreed with my boss about the best place to put the new computer.*
If people have a **difference of opinion**, they disagree politely about a subject: *My teacher and I have a difference of opinion about homework.*

 **marry / get married / be married**
Marry is a transitive verb, so it always takes an object: *My sister married a guy from Colombia.*
Get married is an intransitive verb (no object) referring to an event: *They got married in Bogotá.*
Be married refers to the state: *They've been married for three years now.*

Review: Units 7–9

1 LANGUAGE CHECK

Write the correct form of the item in parentheses.

1. I think shoppers should refuse _____to buy_____ clothes that were made in sweatshops. (buy)
2. That history book, _____ is very interesting, cost only $5. (*a relative pronoun*)
3. By 9:00, I _____ cleaning every room in my apartment, and I felt pretty tired. (finish)
4. My friend Jana, _____ has four cats, is getting a dog. (*a relative pronoun*)
5. Most people tend _____ their New Year's resolutions after just a few days. (break)
6. Aisha realized she _____ when she couldn't find her gold necklace. (be robbed)
7. When I got home, my parents _____ to bed and the house was quiet. (go)
8. The hotel _____ we stayed in had a private beach. (*a relative pronoun*)
9. Jeff couldn't find the theater, and the movie _____ by the time he got there. (start)
10. If the earth's temperature keeps _____ hotter, some small island countries might disappear. (get)
11. The actor _____ made that movie won a lot of awards. (*a relative pronoun*)
12. After I take a big exam, I can't help _____ until I see my grade. (worry)
13. I _____ really hungry after class yesterday because I hadn't eaten all day. (be)
14. I'm from Santiago, _____ is the capital of Chile. (*a relative pronoun*)
15. Yong-Min hopes _____ a degree in computer engineering at a Canadian university. (earn)

2 VOCABULARY CHECK

Match the correct information to make true statements that illustrate the meaning of the words in blue.

1. If you are isolated, ___
2. A legitimate excuse ___
3. If you get out of debt, ___
4. An opportunity ___
5. A fundamental change ___
6. An offense ___
7. If you splurge, ___
8. If you get away with something, ___
9. An extended family ___
10. If you are behind bars, ___
11. If you clash with someone, ___
12. Your upbringing ___
13. If you make ends meet, ___
14. A benefit ___
15. If you bring up children, ___

a. is another word for a crime.
b. is one that is basic and important.
c. is one that is allowed by rules or law.
d. you have enough money to live.
e. you don't owe money for anything.
f. you are in prison.
g. you spend money for luxuries.
h. is a valuable service or privilege given to an employee by an employer
i. you are not punished for doing it.
j. you take care of them until they are grown.
k. is a chance to do something.
l. is the way your parents raised you.
m. you are far from your friends and family.
n. is one that includes many relatives.
o. you have a serious disagreement.

3 NOW YOU'RE TALKING!

Situation 2

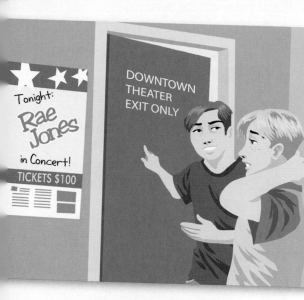

Situation 3

A Pair work. Choose one of the pictures and imagine yourselves in the situation. What would the people talk about? Briefly review the language notes from Units 7–9.

B Pair work. Read the statements in C and add two of your own goals. Then role-play the situation you chose keeping your speaking goals in mind.

C Now rate your speaking. Use + for good, ✓ for OK, and – for things you need to improve.

How did you do?	
I spoke loudly enough for my partner(s) to hear me.	
I spoke without too much hesitation.	
I spoke at a good rate of speed—not too fast or too slow.	
I used new vocabulary from the units.	
I used at least three expressions from the units.	
I practiced the grammar from the units.	
My own goals: 1. _____ 2. _____	

Travel & Vacation

Lesson A | Trips & travel plans

1 VOCABULARY FOCUS

Getting away from it all

 Imagine that you could take a trip around the world. List five places you would absolutely visit. What is one place you would avoid? Share your list with a partner.

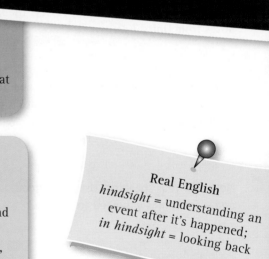

A Both Gavin and Gerald visited the Grand Canyon on separate trips. Read about their experiences. Who had a better time?

GAVIN: The view from the rim of the canyon is absolutely breathtaking. It was so beautiful I was speechless. Up at the rim of the canyon it can get pretty crowded. However, down on the canyon floor it feels pretty desolate—it's a big area and there aren't many people around. Our camping conditions were pretty basic. I felt like I was really roughing it on my own. And yet, I always felt safe accompanied by our two very knowledgeable guides. I love to wander off the beaten path.

You never know what you will find when you explore new areas. I've had many forgettable vacation experiences, but this doesn't fit that category. It was definitely the most memorable vacation of my life.

GERALD: First of all, no one told me the Grand Canyon is in such a remote location—it's so far away and difficult to get to. Despite this fact, it was still overrun with tourists. There was no privacy! As a seasoned traveler, I've been all over the world, but I've never had to live in such primitive conditions for three weeks. We had to sleep outside in tents! Every day was a run-of-the-mill experience: Get up, eat bad food, get in the boat, and float for a few hours. No big deal. In hindsight, I wish I'd never booked this vacation. I blew so much money on this trip when I could've gone somewhere better!

> **Real English**
> *hindsight* = understanding an event after it's happened;
> *in hindsight* = looking back

B Pair work. The definitions below are all *incorrect*.
Correct them with a partner so that each definition is accurate.

> beautiful

1. A view that is *breathtaking* is very ~~hard to see~~.
2. *Desolate* means dangerous.
3. *Roughing it* means spending a lot of money.
4. When you *wander off the beaten path*, you visit familiar places.
5. A *memorable* vacation is a strenuous one.
6. A *remote* location is a crowded one.
7. If a place is *overrun with tourists*, it is affordably priced.
8. A *seasoned traveler* is going on a trip for the first time.
9. *Primitive* means fancy.
10. A *run-of-the-mill* experience is an exciting one.
11. To *book* a trip means to cancel it.
12. When you *blow money*, you exchange it.

>>> Vocabulary Builder ▲

Which words are used to describe travelers, tours, and flights? Categorize each word on a separate piece of paper. (Some words can fit in more than one category.) Then use the words to complete the sentences.

charter	guided	nonstop	turbulent
experienced	adventurous	sightseeing	whirlwind

1. We went on a five-day __sightseeing__ tour and visited all the famous sites.
2. It was a real _____ tour. We saw seven countries in nine days!
3. Our flight was _____ because of the storm. I was relieved when we landed safely on the ground.
4. I don't like _____ tours. I prefer to wander off the beaten path by myself.
5. An _____ traveler knows how to avoid those places that are overrun with tourists.
6. We've booked a special _____ flight for our group. It's not on the regular schedule.
7. Normally when you fly from Seattle to London, you have to stop in New York. But this time, we got a _____ flight and arrived in England sooner.
8. Ari is an _____ traveler who trekked across Europe and Africa by himself last year.

2 LISTENING
There and back again

Real English
fend for oneself = take care of oneself without outside help

A Listen to this interview with Nickolas Alexis about his recent trip. Check the answer that best describes the main purpose of his trip. (CD Tracks 31 & 32)

☐ to visit his relatives   ☐ to make money   ☐ to see the world

B Listen again and complete Nickolas' answers to the questions. (CD Track 33)

1. Q: Where did you start your trip?
   A: First, I went to _____ because I could work there teaching English.

2. Q: What made you take the trip in the first place?
   A: I couldn't _____.

3. Q: How were you able to afford the trip?
   A: I borrowed some money from _____.

4. Q: What's the hardest part about taking an extended round-the-world trip?
   A: You can't avoid _____.

5. Q: Is there anything you wish you had done differently?
   A: I wish I'd done a better job of _____.

▶ **Ask & Answer**
Describe a memorable trip or vacation you took.

C Did Nickolas enjoy doing these things? Circle *yes* or *no*. Give reasons that support your answers. You can infer (conclude) something is true even if Nickolas didn't say so directly.

1. living at home before the trip   Yes   No
   _____

2. living in Greece   Yes   No
   _____

3. working as an English teacher   Yes   No
   _____

4. taking a boat trip on the Amazon   Yes   No
   _____

A Read these two conversations and answer the questions below.

Conversation 1
A: Oh no! Our flight is delayed.
B: Let's ask the gate agent about it . . .
   Excuse me, do you know when our flight will depart?

Conversation 2
A: Oh no! Our flight is delayed.
B: Let's ask the gate agent about it . . .
   Excuse me, when will our flight depart?

1. Look at the question asked in each conversation. Which question form is more polite?
2. What do you notice about the word order of the two questions?

B Study the chart. Then read the conversation below and underline the embedded questions.

Direct questions	Embedded questions
Direct *Wh-* questions	Noun clauses beginning with *Wh-* words
How big is his apartment? When is the party starting?	Do you know <u>how big his apartment is</u>? I'd like to find out <u>when the party is starting</u>.
Direct *Yes/No* questions	Noun clauses beginning with *if/whether*
Have you booked your room yet? Is this a nonstop flight?	I was wondering <u>if you've booked your room yet</u>. Can you tell me <u>whether or not this is a nonstop flight</u>?

- Embedded questions are a type of noun clause.
- Unlike other question forms, embedded questions use statement word order.
- When we ask for information, we can use embedded questions to sound more polite.

Sam: Do you know <u>if we get the train from Seoul to Pusan here</u>?
Tracy: Yeah, I think so.
Sam: I wonder how much the tickets are.
Tracy: I'm not sure. Let's ask. *(speaking to clerk)* Excuse me, can you tell me how much a train ticket from Seoul to Pusan is?
Clerk: 15,000 won.
Tracy: And do you know when the next train is?
Clerk: At 3:30.
Tracy: OK. Oh, one more thing. Do you have any idea if there are any places to stay near the train station in Pusan?
Clerk: Sorry, I'm not sure if there are or not. Ask someone at the information booth when you arrive.

C Complete these sentences that Sam and Tracy said on their train trip by rewriting the information in parentheses in embedded form.

1. The conductor is making an announcement over the intercom, but I can't hear _what he is saying_. (What is he saying?)

2. There's a lot of noise outside. I wonder _____. (What is it?)

3. I'd like to know _____. Our departure has already been delayed an hour. (Is our train departing soon?)

4. I can't remember _____. (What is our estimated time of arrival?)

5. We need to find out _____. (Do they serve meals on this train?)

6. This train usually isn't crowded, but today it's overrun with tourists. I wonder _____. (Why is it so crowded?)

7. In hindsight, this wasn't such a good deal. Maybe they can refund our tickets. Do you know _____? (Are these tickets refundable?)

D Pair work. Role-play a traveler booking a vacation with a travel agent. Decide who will be Student A and who will be Student B and follow the steps below.

1. Student A: Complete the information in the "Vacation Plans" box. Leave three lines blank.
2. Student B: Use the phrases at the bottom of the "Travel Information" box to ask Student A polite questions about his/her travel plans.
3. Student A: Respond to B's questions. Use the phrases at the bottom of your box when responding to questions about the items you left blank.

Student A: Vacation plans
Where: _____
Number of people: _____
Date of departure: _____
Date of return: _____
Preferred airline: _____
Meal preferences: _____
Aisle or window seat: _____
Type of hotel: _____
Smoking or non-smoking room: ____
Airport transportation: Yes   No
Answering questions about travel plans (when you're not sure)
I'm not sure . . .
I don't know . . .
I don't have any idea . . .

Student B: Travel information
Where are you going? _____
How many people are traveling? _____
When are you going? _____
When are you returning? _____
What is your preferred airline? _____
Do you have any meal preferences? _____
What is your seat preference (aisle or window)? _____
What type of hotel would you prefer? _____
What's your smoking preference? _____
Will you need airport transportation? _____
Asking about travel plans
Can/Could you tell me . . . ?
Do you have any idca . . . ?
Do you know . . . ?

> Could you tell me how many people are traveling?

> Two, just my wife and I.

> Do you have any idea when you are going?

> I'm not sure. When is a good time to go to . . .

E Think of three places in your city, and imagine that you need information about them. Write your questions below.

1. _Do you know if Wonderland Amusement Park is open on Sundays?_
2. _____
3. _____
4. _____

F Pair work. Take turns asking and answering the questions in E with a partner.

A Read these conversations. Notice the expressions in blue.

1.   Julio: Have you guys decided how you're going to spend spring break?
     Dave: Well, **what we have in mind is** scuba diving in Belize.
     Julio: Fantastic! I did that two years ago.
     Dave: Really? Do you know where we could stay?
     Julio: Well, **one option** is a beach resort. **Another option** is staying aboard a boat.

2.   Anna: What are you doing for your boyfriend's birthday?
     Katie: **I'm considering** a big dinner party for all our friends.
     Anna: I wonder if that's such a good idea . . .
     Katie: Why?
     Anna: **Considering** the size of your apartment, you might be better off going to a restaurant.

3.   Rie: So, tell me about your trip.
     Bill: **Here's the plan.** We're going to climb Mt. Fuji, sleep at the top, and come down the next day.
     Rie: Uhh . . . **Keep in mind that** it gets cold at night!
     Bill: Well, lots of people climb it every year.

B List the phrases in the appropriate box below.

Here's the plan/idea.   What we have in mind is . . .
Considering that . . .   Keep in mind that . . .
One option is . . . Another option is . . .   I'm considering . . .

Explaining a plan	Taking things into consideration

C Pair work. Discuss these situations. What decisions need to be made?

1. You are starting to plan your wedding. You want to have it on a beach in Hawaii.

2. You want to take a year off to travel.

D Pair work. Role-play the situations in C. One partner explains the plan. The other gives ideas to consider.

Travel & Vacation

Lesson B | Where would *you* go?

1 GET READY TO READ

Taking time off

 How often do you take time off from work or school? What are your usual reasons for doing so? (illness, travel, appointments, etc.)

A Read the question and the four responses below. Pay attention to the words in blue. Which person are you most similar to? Why?

Q: If you could **take time off** from school or work for several months, what would you do?

Miguel

I'd fill my backpack with a week's worth of clothes and **bum around** Europe for a summer. I wouldn't make any particular travel plans—once I got there, I'd decide where to go. Whenever I'd get bored with a place, I'd go somewhere else.

Kira

I'd definitely use the time constructively in some way. I'd take a class and learn a new skill, or maybe I'd fix up my apartment.

Jin Hee

I'd probably stay close to home, and take it easy. You know—I'd just rest: get up late every day and hang out with my friends.

Aaron

I'm pretty busy with work and I'm always **putting off** going to the gym. I haven't been in the last six months. So if I had time off, I'd probably use it to work out and get in shape.

B Complete each sentence by circling the correct word or phrase.

1. If you *take time off* from something, you start / stop doing it forever / for a period of time.
2. Mario is the first person I turn to when I need *constructive* advice. His suggestions are always so useful / unrealistic.
3. After graduating from college, Allison is planning to *bum around* South America for a few months. She has / doesn't have definite travel plans.
4. On her last vacation to Mexico, Gloria *took it easy.* She was busy sightseeing / relaxed on the beach every day.
5. Leo has *put off* writing his paper for our English class, and now he is almost finished / has to write the entire paper tonight.

> **Ask & Answer**
> Have you (or someone you know) ever taken an extended period of time off from school or work? What did you do?

Do any of the following describe you

> I've just graduated from high school, but I don't know what I want to study in college.

> I have another year before I take the university entrance exam.

> I've just graduated from college but am not sure what I want to do with my life.

> I've already got a full-time job, but wish I could change careers.

If you answered "yes" and are feeling a bit uncertain about your future, why not consider taking a "gap year" to think about what you'd like to do next?

A Pair work. Read the ad. What do you think a "gap year" is? Discuss your ideas with a partner. Then read the first section of the article on page 123 to check your answer.

B Study the box to the right. Read the first paragraph of the article on page 123 and the question near it. Then read the rest of the article and write a question after each paragraph that will help you remember the main idea(s).

C Pair work. With a partner, compare the questions you wrote while you read. Then take turns asking and answering the questions.

Writing questions to understand and remember

When you read, it can be helpful to write a question or two next to each paragraph (in your own words) that asks about the main idea(s) discussed in the paragraph.

Asking questions while you read can help you to understand and remember the material better—especially if you are dealing with longer or more difficult texts.

D Complete the chart below with information about each person's gap year.

	What they did	Why they did it	Future plans
Masayuki			
Lexie			

▶ Ask & *Answer*

What do you think about the idea of a gap year? Do you think it's useful? Why or why not? If you could do a gap year, where would you go and what would you do there?

HOME • STORIES • JOIN • LOG IN • HELP • CONTACT

●● *Into the gap*

What was a gap year originally?

The gap year

The term *gap year* originated in Britain. Traditionally, it referred to a specific time between high school and college when a person took time off (a year) from school. The year was spent traveling around and learning about the world—before one began his or her university studies. Today, though, a "gap year" can refer to any time spent away from work or school in pursuit of an interest or a dream. What makes a gap year different from just going on vacation is that a person is involved in some kind of constructive activity. In other words, a gap year isn't an excuse for taking time off to "do nothing." People have spent gap years doing everything imaginable: living on a cruise ship in the Caribbean to learn about the tourism industry, studying art history in Florence, or leading tours across the Serengeti in Africa. The possibilities are endless.

Now, you may be thinking "But I'm not 18 years old." or " I don't have a year to take off." The good news is that the gap experience can take anywhere from one month to a year, and isn't limited only to recent high school graduates. Nowadays, even established professionals who are considering a career or life change are taking time off for a gap year. In addition to being a great adventure, a gap experience can also be an excellent addition to one's résumé.

Snowboarding in the Rockies

Masayuki Sakai, 23, decided to put off going to graduate school to pursue his passion for snowboarding. "You know, I worked pretty hard in college and was ready for a bit of a break," says Masayuki. "At the same time, I didn't want to just bum around for several months without any sort of directions." Instead, Masayuki enrolled in a three-month snowboarding instructor's course in the Canadian Rockies. "Classes were about 20 hours a week," he explains. "In addition, we also did a week-long survival course, which included trekking through the winter forest and spending a couple of nights in remote snow caves in the mountains. It was pretty amazing."

And now that he's completed the course and gotten his level-two certificate, Masayuki is able to work as a snowboard instructor just about anywhere in the world. So, what's next for him? "Well, first, I'll probably send off my applications for graduate school. I feel like I'm ready to do that now. Then, June through early September, I'm hoping to be able to work at a winter resort down in New Zealand for the season to earn some money before starting school again. And who knows . . . if I really love it there, I might stay a while."

Life on a Norwegian farm

Born and raised in Sydney, Australia, Lexie Norfolk, 34, was working as a tax accountant when she decided to take time off to spend six months as a farmhand in Norway. "I'd been thinking about a career change for a while—I really wanted to do something in the food industry—but I wasn't quite sure how to begin. Then I read an article online about people doing "career gaps" and decided to explore that possibility.

"I'd lived my whole life in a city," says Lexie, "so the idea of living and working on a farm in Norway seemed exotic . . . you know, quite different from what I'd been doing, but still, related to food." Turns out that the experience was harder than she expected. "I lived with a host family in a small village in the southwestern part of Norway. I worked about six to seven hours a day, five days a week, doing things like caring for the animals, picking fruit, and harvesting vegetables. It was difficult work, but I had the opportunity to learn just what it takes to produce, harvest, and prepare the food we eat." Back in Australia, Lexie is planning to return to school to study sustainable agriculture. She credits her experience in Norway with helping her to make informed decisions about her new career path.

Getting started on your gap year

So, how can you begin? There is a wealth of information on the web and in bookstores about gap-year experiences. Whatever your plans, a gap year is a wonderful chance to meet people, learn new skills, and explore the world. Many return from a gap experience more self-confident and clearer about their life goals. So, what are you waiting for?

3 WRITING
Writing complaint letters

A Read the tips for writing complaint letters.

B Pair work. Discuss these situations with your partner. What's the problem? To whom could you write a complaint letter? What would you include in the letter?

C On your last vacation, you stayed at the Silver Sea Resort, but you were very disappointed. Look at the ad and the picture and write a letter to the hotel's manager, Randall McLean.

Come to the Silver Sea Resort in beautiful Southville, Florida!

* fabulous ocean views
* quiet, relaxing surroundings
* all rooms newly redecorated
* enjoy our own private beach

One week with all meals and activities just **$1059!**

D Pair work. Exchange letters. Give your partner suggestions to make his or her letter more effective.

If I were you, I'd ask the manager to . . .

The top five

A Look at the list below. Which spot would you like to go to? Why?

THIS WEEK'S TOP FIVE HOT NIGHT SPOTS IN REYKJAVIK, ICELAND

1. **Prikid:** hip nightclub that stays open until 5:30 A.M. on Fridays and Saturdays.
2. **The Blue Lagoon:** Located in a large lava field about 30 minutes outside Reykjavik, these open-air hot springs are a great place to visit after a night out clubbing. Relax in the spring's steamy waters with a drink of your choice.
3. **Perlan:** This revolving restaurant overlooks Reykjavik and offers breathtaking views of the city. Its four-star dinner menu features reindeer appetizers and a variety of fresh fish dishes.
4. **Kaffibarinn:** This cozy candle-lit café transforms into a dance club after midnight and stays open until the early hours of the morning.
5. **Broadway Hotel Iceland:** At this upscale restaurant, patrons are served dinner by up-and-coming actors, musicians, and singers.

B Pair work. With your partner, design a "top-five list" for your city or region. Use one of the ideas from the box or think of your own.

> Top five . . .
> - hot night spots
> - must-see places for tourists
> - places to window shop
> - places to "people watch"
> - most romantic spots
> - places to grab a quick bite to eat
> - places to listen to music
> - other: _____

C Group work. Get together with two other pairs and share your lists. Are there other ideas you could add to their top-five lists?

D Pair work. Take one of the roles below and follow the directions.

Student A: Imagine that you're a visitor to your city and are looking for something interesting to do. Choose a category from the box in B, and ask your partner about:

- the best place to go
- where it is and how to get there
- prices
- hours / best time to go

Student B: You're the concierge at the hotel where your partner is staying. Answer his or her questions.

> *Can you suggest a place where I can go to have a nice meal? You know, a place where the locals go—not one overrun with tourists.*

> *Absolutely. There's a great place nearby called . . .*

E Pair work. Switch roles and do D again.

Unit 10: Travel & Vacation

Expansion Pages

A Complete the sentences with words from the box. Add articles (*a*, *an*, *the*) where needed.

> traveling salesperson   travel agency   travel guide   travelogue
> traveler's checks   travel expenses   widely traveled

1. I usually buy my plane tickets at _____ because I like to get personal advice.
2. Janet always brings _____ with her on vacation because, if they are stolen, you can get your money back.
3. My boss paid for my _____ when I went to the conference in Rome last year.
4. Markos is really _____. I think he's been to more than thirty countries.
5. Last night there was _____ about Argentina on TV. It was really interesting, and there were some great scenes of Buenos Aires.
6. I went to the bookstore and bought a _____ for my trip to Africa.
7. My company has one _____ who shows our new products to customers all over Asia.

B Look at the paragraph below, paying attention to the underlined adjectives that end in –*ed* and –*ing*. Then circle the form of each word to complete the sentences below.

> Even though I'm a <u>seasoned</u> traveler, I certainly wasn't prepared for the weather in Lapland in January: only six hours of sunlight a day and an average temperature of –12 degrees Celsius. With such <u>breathtaking</u> scenery, however, I soon forgot all about it. I was <u>intrigued</u> by all the reindeer and wondered how they could survive in such a cold place. My two favorite things were the Northern Lights and the local spa. Seeing the Northern Lights was <u>thrilling</u>! And whenever I felt tired, a trip to the spa invigorated me. Afterwards, I felt like a new man. When I got home, I was <u>exhausted</u> but very <u>relaxed</u>!

1. I always start my day with a (relaxed / relaxing) early-morning swim.
2. I'm (intrigued / intriguing) by his comments. What do you think they mean?
3. The flight from Los Angeles to Sydney is an (exhausted / exhausting) one. It takes at least 13 hours.
4. We were absolutely (thrilled / thrilling) to visit Lapland. It's been a dream of ours for a long time.

> **I didn't know that!**
> The English word *travel* comes from *travail*, the French word for "work." In the past, travel was not easy and relaxing, but hard work. It took a lot of effort to walk somewhere, and riding on a horse or in a cart was slow and uncomfortable.

C Review the meaning of these words from "Into the Gap" on page 123. Then use the correct form of each word to complete the sentences.

> established (para 2)   passion (para 3)   trekking (para 3)   harvest (para 6)
> sustainable (para 6)   specific (para 1)   pursuit (para 1)

1. Last year, we went _____ in Nepal. We hiked through remote mountain areas for ten days to learn about the culture and environment there.
2. Before he became a teacher, Professor Choi had _____ a career in business.
3. You don't have to finish this project at a _____ time. You can do it whenever you want.
4. Cooking is her _____. She spends every vacation taking courses at famous cooking schools.
5. In my country, people still _____ fruit and other crops by hand. It's very slow work.
6. The police car raced down the street in _____ of the bank robbers.
7. _____ farming doesn't harm the environment, and it can continue for a long time.

D Study the word combinations and use the correct forms of the phrases to complete the sentences. Add articles (*a, an, the*) where needed.

Word combinations with *vacation*			
on vacation	summer/winter vacation	vacation spot	vacation home
take a vacation	family vacation	a two-week/five-day vacation	paid vacation

1. Risa is out of the office this week. She's _____.
2. In our country, all workers receive three weeks of _____ every year, by law.
3. Jeju Island is a very popular _____ for people in Korea.
4. I'm taking a short, _____. I'll be gone Monday, Tuesday, and Wednesday.
5. Kids love to go to Disney World. It's a great place for _____.
6. I really need to _____! I've been working hard for almost a year with very little time off.
7. For my _____, I want to go skiing at Black Mountain.
8. Dr. Rodriguez owns a small house at the beach. He doesn't live there—he just uses it as _____.

In Other Words

A **trip** means traveling to a place: *I took a trip to Tokyo to see my sister.*
A **journey** is a long trip. The word is more commonly used in British English: *It was a long, slow journey from Moscow to Beijing by train.*
A **crossing** is a short trip by water: *The crossing takes an hour.*
A **voyage** is a long trip by sea: *The voyage across the Atlantic used to take two weeks.*
An **excursion** is a short trip for sightseeing: *The tour includes an excursion to White Beach.*

A **ticket** is a piece of paper that allows you to travel on a bus, train, etc.: *I bought a ticket to Bangkok.*
A **pass** is a card that allows you to travel for a certain period of time: *A weekly bus pass costs $5.*
A **token** is a piece of metal that you use instead of money or a ticket: *Put the token in the machine when you get on the bus.*

Watch out!
travel and trip
As a noun, *travel* is uncountable. Use *trip* as a countable noun.
   I've been on three trips to Brazil.
   I've been on three ~~travels~~ to Brazil.

Men & Women

Lesson A | An ideal date

1 VOCABULARY FOCUS

An eligible bachelor

 Imagine that you are going on a date. You have an unlimited amount of money and one afternoon to spend it. What would you do for your date?

A Read this ad for a TV dating show. Who would you pick for Adam? Why?

THIS WEEK'S HIGHLIGHTS

Channel 3 @ 8ₚ

THE WORLD'S BEST CATCH

We went on a search for the most **eligible bachelor** we could find—in short, we were looking for the World's Best Catch! After an exhausting search, we found him **browsing** in an antique bookstore: He's Adam Hunt, 32, from Melbourne, Australia. A spokesperson for a major record label, Adam enjoys an active lifestyle. His future wife should enjoy the same.

"We should be **compatible**. If we don't have similar interests, what's the point?" he asks. Adam adds, "I'm looking for a woman who isn't afraid to live life fully . . . someone who has an **uninhibited** and free spirit," he says.

Adam wasn't exactly eager to join our show to find his future wife. In fact, he was very **reluctant** to try something unusual. "I'm usually in control . . . I'm used to **calling the shots**. And, my last girlfriend **cheated on** me. I didn't want to relive that experience on TV."

Everything changed, though, when Adam read the profiles of the women from our show. "Any of these women would make an **ideal** choice: they're all intelligent, talented, and beautiful. I can't wait."

Read these highlights from Adam's first dates with these women! Who will Adam pick for his second date? Watch tonight and find out!

Celeste

Sylvie

Mina

Isabel

"It rained, so we had our picnic indoors. It was silly and fun. After the date he walked me home in the rain. He was a little too overprotective of me—which is a real turnoff for me."

"There was a lot of chemistry between Adam and me when we first met. At dinner, I couldn't eat anything on the menu because I'm a strict vegetarian. That didn't go over too well with Adam."

"Our date wasn't exactly what I wanted to do. As the sun set, we watched some fireworks. Later we lit a bonfire and roasted marshmallows. We hit it off right away, but unfortunately I got a stomachache from the marshmallows!"

"We went museum-hopping and I got a big headache, but that didn't matter because I fell head over heels in love with Adam—I've already decided that he's the perfect man for me."

B Match the expressions from page 128 with their definitions.

1. eligible _____
2. bachelor _____
3. browsing _____
4. compatible _____
5. uninhibited _____
6. reluctant _____
7. call the shots _____
8. cheat on _____
9. ideal _____
10. chemistry _____
11. not go over well _____
12. hit it off _____
13. fall head over heels _____

a. meet for the first time and immediately like each other
b. looking around a store
c. the way two people relate to each other
d. hesitant
e. secretly have a relationship with another person
f. a single man
g. not well received (by another person)
h. free and unrestrained in behavior
i. available for dating
j. perfect
k. having similar tastes or interests
l. fall in love completely
m. control the situation

▶ **Ask & Answer**

Would you consider going on a reality show like "The World's Best Catch"? Why or why not? Would you recommend it for anyone? If so, whom?

▶▶▶ Vocabulary Builder ▲

A. The work roles of men and women are changing in society and the English language is reflecting this change. Match the old job titles on the left with their new ones on the right.

1. foreman _____
2. postman _____
3. stewardess _____
4. fireman _____

a. flight attendant
b. mail carrier
c. firefighter
d. supervisor

B. What are the current titles for these jobs?

policeman   actress
salesman   waiter/waitress

2 LISTENING
Don't talk about that!

▶ **Ask & Answer**

Have you (or someone you know) ever been on a blind date? How was it? If you haven't been on a blind date, would you go on one? Why or why not?

Real English
foot the bill (for something)
= pay for something

A Which topics do you think are OK to talk about on a first date? Which should be avoided? Make two lists.

Topics OK to talk about: _____   Topics to avoid: _____

B Listen. Jesse and Ashley are on a blind date (they've never met before). What do they talk about on their date? Check (✓) the boxes. (CD Tracks 34 & 35)

1. ☐ apartments
2. ☐ jobs
3. ☐ hobbies
4. ☐ past dating experiences
5. ☐ pets
6. ☐ politics
7. ☐ previous boy/girlfriends
8. ☐ salaries

C Listen again. Circle whether the phrase describes Ashley (A), Jesse (J), or someone else (S). For one item, there is more than one answer. (CD Track 36)

1. likes a job with flexibility   A   J   S
2. short-distance runner   A   J   S
3. dog owner   A   J   S
4. thirty minutes late   A   J   S
5. had to pay for dinner   A   J   S
6. was stood up   A   J   S
7. forgot a date   A   J   S
8. reluctant to go on another date   A   J   S

A Study the sentences in the boxes. Then circle your
answers in the sentences below each box.

Present unreal conditional

My husband and I live in the city. We don't have any children.
If we **had** children, we'd **move** to the suburbs.
(But we don't have children, so we won't move to the suburbs.)

I love Johnny Depp. If I ever **met** him, I'd **ask** him **out** on a date.
(But I've never met him, so I won't ask him out on a date.)

Unreal conditional clauses

if clause = *if we had children*
result clause = *we'd move to the suburbs*

---

1. We use the present unreal conditional to talk about present or future situations that are probable / improbable.
2. In the *if* clause, the verb is in the simple past / past perfect. Use *would* / *would have* + verb in the result clause.
3. In the first example in the box above, the contraction *we'd* means *we had* / *we would*.

Past unreal conditional

My husband and I live in the city. We never had any children.
If we'd **had** children, we **would've moved** to the suburbs.
(But we didn't have children, so we didn't move to the suburbs.)

I went to the Oscars last year. If I'd **seen** Johnny Depp, I **would've taken** his picture.
(But I didn't see him, so I didn't take his picture.)

---

4. We use the past unreal conditional to talk about situations that happened / didn't happen in the past.
5. In the *if* clause, the verb is in the simple past / past perfect. Use *would* / *would have* + verb in the result clause.
6. In the first example in the box above, the contraction *we'd* means *we had* / *we would*.

B Herb and Hilda were recently married. Read what they said about the night they met.
Then read the statements and circle *True* or *False*.

1. **Herb:** If I had gone to a different café that night, I wouldn't have met her.

   Herb went to a different café.   True   False

2. **Hilda:** If I hadn't lost my job and gone to the café to relax, I wouldn't have seen him.

   Hilda didn't lose her job.   True   False

3. **Herb:** If she hadn't smiled at me, I wouldn't have asked her out.

   First Herb asked Hilda out, and then she smiled at him.   True   False

4. **Hilda:** If he had lived far away, I wouldn't have dated him.

   Hilda lived near Herb.   True   False

5. **Hilda:** If he had been too talkative, I would have been turned off.

   Hilda likes quiet guys.   True   False

6. **Herb:** If the café had been romantic, I wouldn't have liked it.

   Herb is a romantic man.   True   False

C Clark asked five different women to go to a movie. Finally, one accepted his invitation. Read their responses to his invitation and then rewrite each response using a conditional sentence.

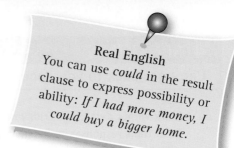

Real English
You can use *could* in the result clause to express possibility or ability: *If I had more money, I could buy a bigger home.*

1. I'm busy, so I can't go.
   If I weren't busy, I could go.

2. My shift at work doesn't end before 10:00, so I can't make it.
   _____

3. My pet bird is sick, so I have to stay home.
   _____

4. My mother doesn't like you, so I'm not allowed to go.
   _____

5. I want to see that movie, so I'll go with you.
   _____

D Pair work. Read Alexis's story below. Then discuss the questions with your partner.

> "I met Peter in May when I was living in Vancouver. We fell head over heels in love. In February the next year, I applied to medical school at Johns Hopkins University—almost 3,000 miles away. To my surprise, I received my acceptance letter in April! Around that same time, Peter received a big job promotion. Also, his mother, who lived nearby, got sick and was hospitalized. Peter felt he couldn't leave his job or his mother, so I moved east to Baltimore alone. We promised to stay in constant contact and to visit as often as we could. Over time, though, we drifted apart. Peter cheated on me, and then I met a very charming med student in Baltimore and we hit it off. Peter and I broke up. Looking back, if things had happened differently . . ."

- What could Alexis and Peter have done differently?
- How might things have been different in their lives if they had acted in another way?

> *I think Alexis made a mistake. If she hadn't applied to medical school so far away, they wouldn't have had a problem in the first place.*

E Pair work. Think of a situation in your life that you have regrets about. What happened? What could you have done differently? How might things have been different in your life if you had acted in another way? Tell a partner.

> *I was in elementary school. I tried to cheat on a test, but I got caught. It was embarrassing, but if I hadn't got caught . . .*

4 SPEAKING

Can I get back to you about that?

Would you like to go bowling with me after work on Friday?

A Mark wants a date for Friday night. He has asked out several women.
Read their responses to his invitation and decide who's interested in going out
with him, who's not interested, and who might be interested.

1. Alison: Let me think about it, OK? _____
2. Mia: I'd love to. What time? _____
3. Sue: Can I get back to you about that later? _____
4. Sachiko: I have to work late. How about another day? _____
5. Erika: Sorry, I'm sure I'm busy then. _____
6. Dalia: Hmmm. I'll have to check my calendar. _____
7. Sun-hee: Sure, sounds good. _____
8. Jennie: I'm afraid I can't. Thanks, though. _____

B How should Mark respond? Match an appropriate response to each person in A.
You may use a response more than once.

a. Oh, OK. Maybe some other time.   d. Great. How about 7:00?
b. Well, let me know if you're free, then. e. What about Saturday?
c. Sure, just let me know.

C What would you like to do on Saturday? Fill in the blanks and rank each of the ideas from
1 (most appealing) to 5 (least appealing).

Ideas for Saturday	Rank
a. go to a lecture about _____	
b. see a _____ movie	
c. have dinner at a _____ restaurant	
d. go to a _____ concert	
e. go to a _____ game	

D Group work. Walk around the class making and responding to invitations for the activities in C.
Try to find one person who will do each activity with you. Accept invitations only for your two
favorite activities, and refuse the others politely.

E Group work. Now imagine that your best friend has just invited you to a great party on Saturday.
Go back to the two people whose invitations you accepted in D and cancel the arrangements.
Give an excuse, but don't tell them about the party!

I'm really sorry, but I can't . . .
I'm afraid I'm not going to be able to . . .
Sorry, something's come up and . . .

World Link

F Pair work. Role-play one of your conversations in E
for the class. What were the best excuses?

Although experts recommend breaking up in person,
many Internet sites are now offering "break-up e-cards"
to end a relationship. It may be bad manners, but it's the
ultimate in convenience!

Men & Women

| *Lesson B* | Breaking up is hard to do. |

1 GET READY TO READ

Commitment issues

You often hear people say "celebrity marriages never last." Why do you think celebrities are always breaking up?

A Pair work. Read the magazine profiles below, paying attention to the words and phrases in blue. Then discuss the questions with your partner.

- What do all three of these people's love lives have in common?
- If you had to use an adjective or two to describe each person, what would you use? Why?

View Magazine   February 12

With Valentine's Day just around the corner, **View Magazine** examines the love lives of three of today's hottest celebrities.

Actress/Singer
Jennifer Sanchez, 24

"I know I've been married twice already, but you know what they say! Three's a charm . . . This time I think I've really found my **soulmate**. Jean-Claude and I are a perfect match. I fell head over heels for him when we met six weeks ago. I'm so happy!"

Oh, no. Here we go again! To learn more about Jen's third trip down the aisle, turn to our story on **page 10.**

Soccer Player
Davy Hambeck, 29

"It's true that Cindy and I have been dating for almost eight years. But why is everyone **pressuring** me to get married? I'm just not that **into it** right now."

Is Davy afraid of **commitment**? Details on **page 12.**

Pop Star
Whitney Spares, 22

"Leo and I have been friends since high school. On Friday night we decided to get married in Las Vegas. It's true that I **dumped** him the next day . . . Everyone is saying that I didn't think about his feelings . . . that I'm totally **insensitive**. Well, what about my feelings?"

Married today, single tomorrow— literally. Whitney gives new meaning to the phrase "love them and leave them." See **page 15.**

▶ **Ask & Answer**

Which article would you most like to read and why? Do you believe in "soulmates"? Do think that there is one right person out there for you?

B Pair work. Look again at the words and phrases in blue in A. What do you think each one means? Discuss your ideas with a partner. If you need additional help, use your dictionary.

2 READING
The Etiquette of Breaking Up

Identifying what to read first

With many texts, it is often helpful to skim the entire reading and to identify which parts are the most important and need to be read carefully. Read these sections first—even if they come later in a text.

When you read a piece a second time, sections that you skimmed can be read more closely for detail.

A Pair work. What are different ways that you can break up with someone? Which are the most common? The least common? Make a list with a partner and then share your ideas with the class.

B Pair work. Read the title of the reading and the definition below. Then in your own words, tell your partner what you think the reading is going to be about.

> *etiquette*: rules for how to behave properly

C Study the box and then look at the reading on page 135. Which parts should you read closely the first time? Which parts could you skim in a first read? Skim and then complete D below.

D According to the author, is it OK to use these methods to break up with someone? Check *Yes* or *No*. For each *yes* answer, explain when the method should be used.

Methods	OK to use?		When should you use this method?
Face-to-face	☐ Yes	☐ No	
Phone	☐ Yes	☐ No	
E-mail/IM	☐ Yes	☐ No	
The silent treatment	☐ Yes	☐ No	

E Read the entire article again closely. Then answer the questions below with information from the reading.

1. How and why did Margo break up with Ben?
   _____

2. What does Ben think of using e-mail or IM to break up with someone? Why?
   _____

3. If you split up with someone face-to-face, what should you think about?
   _____

4. Before you send a break-up message by e-mail or IM, what should you do first?
   _____

5. Why is the silent treatment rarely a good way to split up with someone?
   _____

> **▶ Ask & Answer**
>
> Do you agree with the advice given in the reading? Why or why not? Which method would you use to break up with someone? Why?

Real English
blown away = very surprised
it's up to you = it's your decision or responsibility

The Etiquette of Breaking Up

Ben Hiller, 23, and Margo San Giacamo, 21, had been dating for five months and, by all accounts, appeared to be the perfect couple. "We had a lot in common; you know, we did everything together," recalls Ben. "On our five-month anniversary, we went out to dinner and talked about her meeting my folks. It was a very casual discussion—no pressure involved." Imagine Ben's surprise when, three days later, he checked his e-mail and found a message from Margo telling him that she wanted to break up. "I was completely blown away," says Ben. "I thought that we were soulmates. And then she dumps me . . . by e-mail!"

Margo defends herself. "Yeah, Ben and I had been seeing a lot of each other, it's true. But then I realized that I just wasn't into having a really serious relationship. And I knew that if I told him face-to-face that I wanted to break up, it would've been too hard. E-mail just made everything so simple."

Was Margo's behavior insensitive? Should she have told Ben in person that she wanted to end the relationship? According to Ben, using e-mail to split up with someone is unfair. "If you want to end a relationship, fine. But at least pick up the phone or do it in person. When you e-mail or IM someone and say 'it's over,' it doesn't give the other person a chance to ask questions or even say good-bye to you. It's a totally selfish way of handling things, and that's not cool."

And so, what is the best way to let another person know that you're ready to move on? Is the same approach right for every situation? Read on to learn what one expert has to say about "the etiquette of breaking up."

Taking Care of Business

Face-to-face: If you've been dating someone for a while, be thoughtful and tell him or her in person that the relationship is over. Your future ex deserves to be told face-to-face that you want to break up. Choosing the location for the break-up is up to you. Just be sure to consider your partner's feelings when choosing a spot. If you think he or she may be very emotional, don't meet in a crowded café. Choose a more private location, like a quiet park bench.

Phone: Involved in a long-distance relationship that's not working? Aren't interested in continuing to see someone you've only dated once or twice? In each of these cases, the phone is an acceptable, and perhaps the only way, to end a relationship. Remember: When you end things, be as kind and respectful as possible.

E-mail / Instant Messaging: In the minds of many people, IMing or using e-mail to break up is both impersonal and unkind. But the fact is, sometimes it's the best way to say "good-bye" or "no thanks" to a relationship—especially if you've just met or have only had a relationship online. Before you hit Send, though, read over your message and consider how you'd feel if it were being sent to you.

The silent treatment: Simply avoiding or not contacting someone is almost never a good way to end a relationship. Silence very often sends a clear message (that is, "I don't want to see you anymore"). But for some people, it is an excuse to believe that there is still hope for the relationship to continue. Though it may be difficult, it's better to be honest and tell the other person. After all, you started a relationship with this person. Now it's your responsibility to end it—the right way.

3 WRITING
Formal versus informal e-mails

A Pair work. Discuss these questions.

1. How is an e-mail similar to a letter? A conversation? How is it different from these things?
2. What differences are there in writing an e-mail to a friend / your teacher / a coworker / a company?

B Look at the box. Can you add other suggestions?

Writing better e-mails

- Don't use informal language with people you don't know.
- Use emoticons like :) or :(with friends so they won't misunderstand your meaning.
- _____
- _____

C Read Amy's messages below.

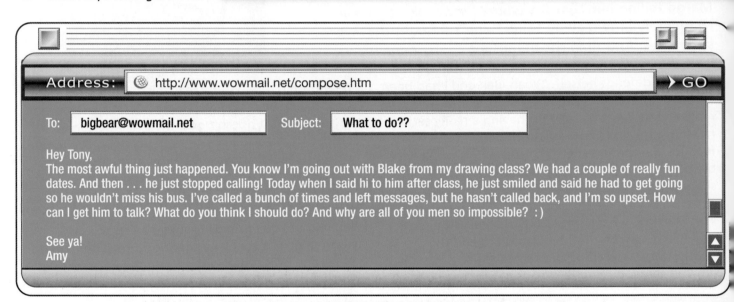

Address: http://www.wowmail.net/compose.htm › GO

To: bigbear@wowmail.net   Subject: What to do??

Hey Tony,
The most awful thing just happened. You know I'm going out with Blake from my drawing class? We had a couple of really fun dates. And then . . . he just stopped calling! Today when I said hi to him after class, he just smiled and said he had to get going so he wouldn't miss his bus. I've called a bunch of times and left messages, but he hasn't called back, and I'm so upset. How can I get him to talk? What do you think I should do? And why are all of you men so impossible? :)

See ya!
Amy

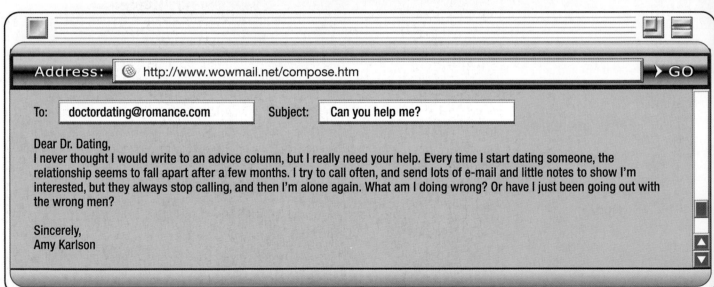

Address: http://www.wowmail.net/compose.htm › GO

To: doctordating@romance.com   Subject: Can you help me?

Dear Dr. Dating,
I never thought I would write to an advice column, but I really need your help. Every time I start dating someone, the relationship seems to fall apart after a few months. I try to call often, and send lots of e-mail and little notes to show I'm interested, but they always stop calling, and then I'm alone again. What am I doing wrong? Or have I just been going out with the wrong men?

Sincerely,
Amy Karlson

D Write an e-mail reply to each message. For the first message, you're Amy's friend. For the second, you're an advice columnist.

E Pair work. Read your partner's messages and make suggestions for clarifying anything that the reader might misunderstand.

Activity 1: Let's imagine . . .

A Read each of the incomplete sentences below and think about how you would finish each one.

1. If I could have dinner with any man or woman, past or present, I'd choose . . .
2. If I were married and later met someone whom I believed was my true soulmate, I'd . . .
3. If I were president of my country for a day, I'd . . .
4. If I'd been born 100 years ago, I probably would've . . .
5. If my life were made into a movie, the theme song of the film would be . . .
6. If I were in love with someone from another country, and the person asked me to move to his or her country, I'd . . .

B Pair work. Take turns sharing your sentences in **A** with a partner. Explain your answers. Ask your partner questions.

C Pair work. With your partner, think of an incomplete "If . . ." sentence, and write your idea on the board.

D Pair work. Read the incomplete sentences on the board from your classmates and discuss with your partner how you would finish each one.

Activity 2: What if we'd never met?

A Think of three people who have had an impact on your life, such as a parent, a friend, a teacher, or your spouse. Complete the chart below about each person.

Person's name and relationship to me	How he or she has influenced my life
1.	
2.	
3.	

B Pair work. Share your ideas in **A** with a partner. Tell him or her how your life would be different now if those people weren't in your life or if you had never met them.

> *My friend Oscar and I have known each other since high school. His sister is my girlfriend. If he and I weren't friends, I probably never would've met her . . .*

 **Check out the CNN® video.** **Practice your English online at elt.heinle.com/worldpass**

Unit 11: Men & Women

Expansion Pages

A What do people like to do on a date? Match the activities with the correct verb. Circle your three favorites.

> go   have   take   see   play

1. _____ coffee on Saturday afternoon
2. _____ dinner at a sushi restaurant
3. _____ a tour of the art museum
4. _____ tennis after work
5. _____ a walk on the beach
6. _____ racquetball at the health club

7. _____ dancing at a new club
8. _____ on a picnic in the park
9. _____ an old comedy movie
10. _____ a new play
11. _____ to a party at a friend's house

B Review the meaning of these words from "The Etiquette of Breaking Up" on page 135. Then use the correct form of each word to complete the sentences.

> impersonal   ex   defend   insensitive   emotional   acceptable   silent

1. Every time I see my _____, I'm so glad I broke up with him. We just start arguing all over again.
2. Many people don't think it's _____ to discuss a serious subject like breaking up in Instant Messaging.
3. He shouldn't have told Megan that she looks fat. That was really _____!
4. I don't like taking large classes. The teacher doesn't even know your name, so it's very _____.
5. When Dave broke up with his girlfriend by e-mail, he _____ himself by saying that it was the quickest way to end the relationship.
6. The girl kept _____ and refused to talk to her boyfriend at all.
7. I got very _____ during the movie—in fact, I started crying.

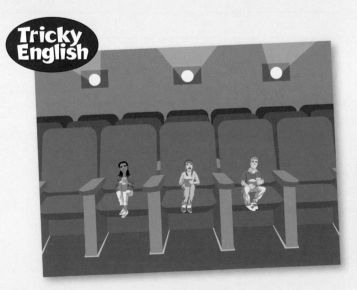

Incorrect: *There were little people at the movie.*   **Correct:** *There were few people at the movie.*

Tricky English

138   Expansion Pages: Unit 11

C Match these sentences about relationships with their meanings.

1. It's a match made in heaven. ___
2. Our marriage is on the rocks. ___
3. I don't know what she sees in him. ___
4. They decided to go their separate ways. ___
5. It just wasn't meant to be. ___
6. The honeymoon is over. ___
7. It was love at first sight. ___

a. They fell in love immediately.
b. They broke up.
c. They've started disagreeing and arguing.
d. They make a perfect couple.
e. I don't understand why she likes him.
f. We're having a lot of problems.
g. The relationship didn't work out.

D Study the word combinations. Use the correct form of them to complete the sentences. Add articles (*a, an, the*) where needed.

Word combinations with *love*		
love song	love child	love-hate relationship
love story	love triangle	be madly in love with
love affair	much loved	

1. The whole family was sad because their _____ dog had run away.
2. I have _____ with my boyfriend. He makes me so angry, but I can't live without him.
3. The movie *Titanic* is about a rich woman who has _____ with a poor, handsome young man, and it changes her life.
4. I heard my favorite old _____ on the radio last night. It made me cry!
5. I read an article in an entertainment magazine all about _____ between a famous comedian and his two girlfriends.
6. My mother read _____ about a princess in her favorite romance magazine, and then called me and told me all the details.
7. Jake _____ Susana. He doesn't want to spend even an hour apart from her!
8. The newspaper said that the company CEO had a secret _____ with his former office assistant. Their son is now three years old.

In Other Words

Your **boyfriend/girlfriend** is the person you're dating: *I met my boyfriend at a party.*
If you are not dating, use **friend**: *This is Juan Carlos. He's my friend from the office.*
To talk about your friends who are men or women, you can say **male friends / female friends**: *Most of my male friends are single.*
Your **fiancé/fiancée** is the person you're planning to marry: *I talked to my fiancé last night about picking a date for our wedding.*
Your **spouse** means your husband or wife: *The company had a party for the sales staff and their spouses.*

fall in love and **be in love**
If you *fall in love*, it's an event that happens at a definite moment:
I fell in love with my boyfriend on our first date.
If you *are in love*, it's a state that continues over time: *How can I tell her I'm not in love with her anymore?*

1 VOCABULARY FOCUS

Be prepared

 What kind of plans does your city or country have in place for natural disasters, such as an earthquake or flood? Do you know where to go in case of an emergency?

A Read these tips about emergency preparedness. How many of these things have you done?

HELP YOUR FAMILY BE PREPARED

The following tips will help your family in case of an emergency:

- Organize **essential** medicines and make sure they're accessible to all members of the family. Don't **jeopardize** your family's health needlessly.

- In addition, keep these items **on hand** at all times: first aid kit, emergency food and water, can opener, cash and credit cards, portable battery-operated radio.

- **Devise** an emergency plan for your family. **Walk through** the plan so that everyone knows what to do. Practice it several times. Discuss a **back-up plan** in case you can't **implement** your original plan during an actual emergency.

- Learn about the early **warning systems** in your community and how they work.

- Memorize important phone numbers. Remember, during an emergency you may experience difficulty in **getting through** to someone because phone lines may be busy. Be patient and keep trying.

- Take the time to learn local **evacuation** routes in case you are forced to leave your home suddenly.

- After a disaster, **take into consideration** the **extent** of the damage before you try to return home. When in doubt, check with local authorities to **evaluate** the situation.

- Order the latest copy of *Be Prepared!*, a government manual that gives **in-depth** information on specific **hazards** (floods, storms, etc.) and what to do when they occur.

B Match the words with their definitions.

a. essential	d. devise	g. implement	j. evacuation	m evaluate
b. jeopardize	e. walk through	h. warning system	k. take into consideration	n. in-depth
c. on hand	f. back-up plan	i. get through	l. extent	o. hazard

1. ___ invent
2. ___ an extra plan
3. ___ detailed
4. ___ study the facts
5. ___ readily available

6. ___ size or amount
7. ___ start using (a plan)
8. ___ rehearse
9. ___ necessary
10. ___ think about

11. ___ make a telephone connection with someone
12. ___ endanger
13. ___ something that is dangerous
14. ___ the process of making people leave an unsafe place
15. ___ a system that gives advance notice about possible danger

C Pair work. If you had to evacuate your home and could take only three items with you, what would you choose and why? Discuss your answers with a partner.

▶ **Ask & Answer**
In general, would you say that you're prepared for an emergency? Why or why not?

▶▶ Vocabulary Builder ▲

A. Complete the chart below.

Verb	Noun	Verb	Noun	Noun	Adjective
jeopardize	jeopardy	evacuate			hazardous
	summary		evaluation	poison	

B. Complete each sentence with one of the words in the chart.

1. Watch out! That snake is _____!
2. If the fire gets too close, we will have to prepare for an _____ of the city.
3. Stay calm during an emergency. If not, you'll be putting your life, and the lives of others, in _____.
4. Smoking is _____ to your health.
5. The government's _____ of the damage didn't include all buildings.

2 LISTENING

It's an emergency!

A Listen. What does Aidan, an emergency dispatcher, do on a typical emergency call? Put the steps in order.
(CD Tracks 37 & 38)

___ get more detailed information
_1_ answer the call
___ get the location
___ send help
___ get the caller's phone number
___ stay on the line
___ decide if the situation is an emergency or not

Real English
be cut out for (something) =
be capable of doing something

Listen again. Complete the information about the two callers. Write *U* if a piece of information is unknown. (CD Track 39)

1. Name of caller: <u>Gretchen Smith</u>

   Location of caller: _____

   Person injured? ☐ yes ☐ no

   Ambulance sent? ☐ yes ☐ no

   Phone number: _____

   Details: _____

2. Name of caller: _____

   Location of caller: _____

   Person injured? ☐ yes ☐ no

   Ambulance sent? ☐ yes ☐ no

   Phone number: _____

   Details: _____

▶ **Ask & *Answer***

Have you (or someone you know) ever called for help in an emergency? What happened?

3 LANGUAGE FOCUS
Reported speech

Using reported speech

The sentences in A are examples of quoted speech. In quoted speech, you write exactly what the speaker said. The sentences in B are examples of reported speech. In reported speech, you change the verb tenses, pronouns, and time expressions (adverbs) to make the speaker's words part of another sentence.

A There was a mud slide on November 20 in the mountains near Cascade Village. Underline what people said about the disaster shortly after it happened.

1. "<u>We're all safe, but we've lost everything</u>," the Palau family said.
2. "We've recorded the wettest month on record here," said Sam Golden.
3. "The rains will taper off and finally stop late tomorrow," said Sam Golden.
4. "Three people are missing," said Ben Chapman.
5. "There's no need to implement a new early warning system," said Ben Chapman.
6. "Five hundred people have been evacuated from their homes," said Emily Ross.
7. "The Red Cross is working to find shelter for these people," said Emily Ross.

B Now read a news article about the mud slide. Underline the examples of reported speech. What differences do you notice between quoted and reported speech?

The Daily News

November 21 (AP) It's been a tough week for everyone, but especially for the residents of Cascade Village, high in the mountains. The heavy rains have triggered mudslides. The Palau family, residents of the village for 15 years, watched helplessly as their home was crushed instantly by a wall of mud. They said <u>they were all safe, but that they'd lost everything</u>.

Sam Golden, Channel 5 weather forecaster, reported that they had recorded the wettest month on record there. He also added that the rains would taper off and finally stop late today.

Ben Chapman and his fire crew were busy digging through the mud. Mr. Chapman said three people were missing. Mr. Chapman added that there was no need to implement a new early warning system because it had worked well.

Red Cross representative Emily Ross said 500 people had been evacuated from their homes, and that the Red Cross was working to find shelter for those people.

C Amy attended a lecture about tornadoes. Read the reported speech.
Then circle the quoted speech that Amy reported.

1. He said that a tornado was a violent windstorm.
   a. "A tornado is a violent windstorm."
   b. "The tornado was a violent windstorm."

2. He said that a tornado had hit the week before. The extent of the damage
   was still unknown.
   a. "A tornado hit last week. The extent of the damage is still unknown."
   b. "A tornado hit last week. The extent of the damage was still unknown."

3. He said the warning time before a tornado strikes could be short.
   a. "The warning time before a tornado strikes is short."
   b. "The warning time before a tornado strikes can be short."

4. He said that many tornadoes hit there, but they don't know when the next
   one would come.
   a. "Many tornadoes hit here, but we don't know when the next one will come."
   b. "Many tornadoes hit there, but we don't know when the next one could come."

D Pair work. Gil overheard pieces of a conversation at a local café and later told a friend. Read sentences 1–5
only and rewrite them as Gil's reported speech. Tell your partner what you think the man and woman were talking about.

1. Woman: We're in a terrible mess. _She said that they were in a terrible mess._

2. Man: I know. It's dead. _____

3. Woman: This jeopardizes all our plans. _____

4. Man: I have to call the boss right now. _____

5. Woman: He's not going to be happy. _____

E Pair work. Now read sentences 6–9 and rewrite them in reported speech.
Tell your partner what the couple was really talking about.

6. Man: I don't understand how it happened. _____

7. Woman: It's because you left the headlights on. _____

8. Man: Maybe we shouldn't tell our boss. He'll be furious. _____

9. Woman: You're right. We need to fix it ourselves. _____

F Pair work. Use one of these ideas to tell your partner about a personal experience.
Use the questions below to help you get started.

- a big storm   • a delay due to an emergency situation   • other: _____
- a blackout   • a scary travel experience

What happened?   How did you feel?   What did you do?

G Pair work. Work with another partner. Tell your new partner what you learned from your first partner.

> Eliza had an amazing story. She was delayed because of a
> subway fire. She said that it was really scary. They were . . .

4 SPEAKING

Everything's going to be OK.

A Both Rick and Julie are facing a crisis. Read the conversations. Then add the expressions in blue to the correct column of the chart.

Conversation 1

Josh:	Hello?
Rick:	Hi, this is Rick . . . Josh, you've got to help me, my computer just crashed! And my paper is due tomorrow morning!
Josh:	Aw, **don't get upset.** I'm sure we can take care of it. **Can you tell me exactly what happened?**
Rick:	I was typing the last page, and suddenly the screen went all blue!
Josh:	**What did you do then?**
Rick:	I just restarted the computer.
Josh:	Well, **why don't you try** finding the back-up folder and looking inside?
Rick:	OK . . .
Josh:	**Did that work?**
Rick:	Yeah! There's my paper! Hey, thanks!

Conversation 2

Mrs. Kang:	Hello?
Julie:	Mom—Tanya, my roommate, just cut her hand. It's bleeding like crazy!
Mrs. Kang:	**Take it easy. What happened?**
Julie:	She was cutting vegetables for a salad and the knife slipped.
Mrs. Kang:	Well, it might not be as bad as it looks. **You need to** put a clean towel on her hand and press down hard.
Julie:	OK . . . I'm doing that . . .
Mrs. Kang:	**Is it any better?**
Julie:	No, not really. It looks like a deep cut.
Mrs. Kang:	Then **you'd better** call 911. And don't worry—everything's going to be OK.

Reassuring someone	Figuring out the situation	Giving a solution	Checking the solution
Don't worry.	What's the matter?	The first/next thing to do is . . .	How is he/she/it now?
Relax.	What does it look/sound like?	You'd better . . .	What's happening now?
Nothing to worry about.	What happened after that?	_____	_____
Hang in there.	Can you tell me exactly what happened?	_____	_____
Take it easy.			
_____	_____		
_____	_____		

B Which expressions would you use for a very serious problem? Why?

C Pair work. Who would you call for help in these situations? Role-play the phone calls with your partner.

1. You're washing your hands at home when an expensive ring falls off your finger and down the drain of the sink.
2. You've just tried a new brand of hair color. An hour later, your head starts to itch, and you see red bumps on your skin.
3. You're at home watching TV when you hear the sound of running water. When you look up, you see a crack in the ceiling and water coming down.

D Pair work. Think of a problem, but don't tell your partner what it is.
Then "call" your partner to ask for help, and work out a solution together.

Emergency!

Lesson B | Natural disasters

1 GET READY TO READ

Early warning systems

 Have you (or someone you know) ever been in an earthquake? Was there any warning that the quake was going to happen? Discuss your answers with a partner.

A Study the box. Then read the paragraphs below. As you read, pay attention to what Dr. Shou and NASA have in common and how they differ.

Comparing and contrasting

When we compare things, we look for similarities. Words and phrases such as *like, also, as with, similarly* are used to signal comparison. When we contrast things, we explore differences. Words and phrases such as *but, however, despite this, nevertheless, though, unlike, whereas* are used to signal a contrast or opposition.

Early Warning Systems

According to one source, almost 500,000 earthquakes occur every year. Approximately one-fifth of these are felt by humans, and between 50 and 100 are strong enough to cause serious damage.

Dr. Zhonghao Shou, a scientist in China, is interested in predicting earthquakes before they happen. He believes it is possible to do this by using an ancient practice of studying clouds. According to this theory, a certain kind of cloud will appear in the sky days before a major quake hits. Dr. Shou says he has used this method to predict several large earthquakes. Many in the scientific community are skeptical about this, though.

Scientists at NASA are also interested in detecting earthquakes before they strike. Like Dr. Shou, they believe that it may be helpful to analyze clouds and other weather patterns. But unlike the Chinese scientist, NASA is using high-tech satellite images to study the weather, as well as changes in temperature and movement along earthquake faults around the globe.

NASA's satellite technology hasn't led to successful predictions yet (whereas Dr. Shou has had some success). Nevertheless, many in the scientific community are hopeful that data sent from space will eventually help us to predict future quakes and prevent loss of life.

B Pair work. To whom do these statements apply? Check (✓) the correct answers below. Then discuss the similarities and differences between Dr. Shou and NASA with a partner.

	Dr. Shou	NASA
1. interested in predicting earthquakes	☐	☐
2. uses high-tech satellites	☐	☐
3. studies weather patterns	☐	☐
4. analyzes earthquake faults	☐	☐
5. predicted some earthquakes	☐	☐
6. has the support of the scientific community	☐	☐

▶ **Ask & Answer**

Which method do you think is more reliable? Why?

2 READING

Recognizing the signs

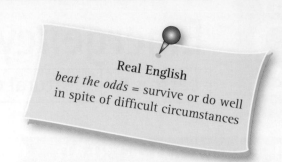

Real English
beat the odds = survive or do well in spite of difficult circumstances

A Read the two stories on page 147. As you read, pay attention to what they have in common and how they differ.

B Complete the chart with information from the two stories.

	Tribespeople, Andaman Islands	Tilly Smith and people on Maikhao Beach
1. Why were they there?	They live there.	
2. Why weren't they warned about the tsunami?		
3. What signs did they notice before the tsunami hit?		
4. Where did they learn to interpret these signs?		
5. Where did they go for protection?		
6. How many of them survived?		

C Pair work. What do the two stories have in common? How are they different? Use the information in the chart in **B** to discuss the similarities and differences with your partner.

D Pair work. Find the following words in the reading and write a possible definition for each with your partner.

1. In line 17, *devastated* means <u>ruined or damaged severely.</u>
2. In line 19, *wiped out* means _____
3. In line 22, *emerged* means _____
4. In line 26, *fled* means _____
5. In line 34, *retreated* means _____

▶ **Ask & Answer**

The people in the two stories beat the odds and survived the terrible events of December 26, 2004. Do you know a story about someone who beat the odds? What happened?

World Link

What's the difference between a typhoon and a hurricane? According to meteorologists, there isn't any! These powerful, swirling storms are called typhoons when they're over the Pacific Ocean, and hurricanes when they're over the Atlantic.

On December 26, 2004, an earthquake registering over 9.0 hit off the coast of Indonesia in the Indian Ocean, triggering an enormous tsunami. The wave destroyed seaside communities and killed hundreds of thousands of people throughout the region in one of the worst natural disasters in modern history. Below are two stories of people who beat the odds and survived the massive wave on that fateful day.

Tribespeople Notice Signs, Escape Danger

Located in the Bay of Bengal, just off the coast of India, are the Andaman and Nicobar Islands. Known for their great beauty, the islands are also home to some of the world's oldest tribes of people (believed by scientists to be almost 70,000 years old)—the Jarawas, Sentinatese, Onges, and the Great Andamanese. These tribespeople continue to depend on nature for their survival by hunting animals and gathering food from the forests. They rarely interact with members of the outside world.

On December 26, the Andaman and Nicobar Islands were devastated by the quake and tsunami. Thousands lost their lives and many more were injured. People assumed that the tribespeople, already very small in number, had been wiped out when the disaster hit.

And then, on the morning of January 6, 2005, members of the Jarawa tribe emerged from the forest, announcing that all of their people were alive. Afterwards, eyewitnesses said that almost no tribespeople had been seen on the beaches in the early morning hours of December 26, despite the fact that they normally fished there at that time of the day. They had fled to higher ground before the wave hit. With no early warning system in place, how did the members of these tribes know to leave the shore and head to higher ground that morning? One scientist interviewed said that their knowledge of changes in the sea and wind enabled them to understand that something unusual, and potentially dangerous, was about to happen. Because the tribes live close to nature, they had recognized the signs and quickly retreated from the coast to nearby forested hills that morning.

Schoolgirl Remembers Lesson, Warns Others

The coast of southern Thailand was also one of the areas hit hard by the tsunami. As with the Andaman and Nicobar Islands, there was no warning following the earthquake that a major tsunami was on its way. 40 Nevertheless, vacationers on one of Thailand's most popular beaches escaped unharmed that day—thanks to a British schoolgirl visiting with her family.

On the morning of December 26, 10-year-old Tilly 45 Smith and her family were relaxing on Maikhao Beach in Phuket in southern Thailand. Though everyone had been surprised by the earthquake that morning, many had chosen to get on with the day and enjoy themselves. Tilly, however, felt that something wasn't quite right. The water, she noticed, had 50 begun to bubble and move back from the shore. As she watched this happen, she kept thinking about a geography lesson she'd had in school just before the December break. In that class, Tilly had learned about earthquakes and how they can trigger violent tsunamis. Remembering this, Tilly ran and 55 told her mother that they needed to get off the beach . . . immediately. Her warning spread along the shore and within minutes, the beach was deserted. Vacationers ran to a nearby hotel and headed for higher floors just minutes before powerful waves hit the beach and flooded the village. 60

Vacationers on Maikhao Beach escaped with their lives that day, thanks to quick-thinking Tilly Smith. Like the tribespeople of the Andaman Islands, Tilly had recognized nature's warning signs and fled, just in time, to safety.

A Pair work. A magazine article, a sales report, and an essay for a job application are examples of writing that usually has more than one paragraph. Give your partner at least two other examples.

B Read this paragraph and identify the topic sentence, supporting ideas, and conclusion.

> Thunderstorms occur all over the world, and they can be very dangerous. There are several important rules that you should follow during a severe thunderstorm. First, be aware of the weather. Second, if you are caught outdoors, take shelter. Third, be careful indoors during a thunderstorm. If you follow these rules, you can stay safe in any thunderstorm.

C Read the outline in D for a magazine article. Notice the following:

- The topic sentence in B is in the introduction of the article.
- The supporting ideas in B are the topic sentences of the middle paragraphs of the article.
- The conclusion sentence in B is part of the conclusion of the article.

D Turn the paragraph in B into a magazine article by putting the sentences in the box in the correct places in the article.

> Don't use land-line phones, because electricity can pass through the wires.
> Try to get inside a building or a car.
> Avoid taking a bath or shower until the storm has passed.
> ~~Always check the weather forecast before beginning any outdoor activities.~~
> If you see big clouds forming while you are driving, listen for thunder.
> Stay away from big metal objects such as your refrigerator.
> If that's not possible, find a low place away from water.
> Don't stand under a tree, because lightning usually hits the highest target.

Thunderstorms

Thunderstorms occur all over the world, and they can be very dangerous. There are several important rules that you should follow during a severe thunderstorm.

First, be aware of the weather. _Always check the weather forecast before beginning any outdoor activities._
_____

Second, if you are caught outdoors, take shelter.
_____
_____
_____

Third, be careful indoors during a thunderstorm.
_____
_____
_____

If you follow these rules, you can stay safe in any thunderstorm. You may even enjoy its power and beauty.

E Write a short magazine article explaining what people should do in a weather emergency that occurs in your country. Include an introduction, at least two paragraphs with supporting ideas, and a conclusion.

F Pair work. Exchange papers. Check that your partner's article has a clear introduction and conclusion and paragraphs with supporting ideas.

4 COMMUNICATION

Activity 1: Everyday emergencies

A Read about these everyday emergencies and think about what you would do in each situation.

B Pair work. Take turns asking and answering the questions in A with a partner. Explain your answers. Have any of these things ever happened to you or to someone you know?

How would you survive each one of these everyday emergencies?

1. On your way to an important job interview, you get splashed by a taxi. It leaves a big water stain on the front of your clothes. What would you do?
   a. skip the interview
   b. buy a new outfit
   c. go and explain what happened
   d. other _____

2. You're on a first date with someone and it's going terribly. You want to leave. What would you do?
   a. endure the situation
   b. pretend to be ill
   c. go to the rest room and not come back
   d. other _____

3. Your host at a dinner party has just served the main dish. It's a food that you don't like at all. What would you do?
   a. eat it anyway
   b. pretend to be full and decline
   c. say honestly that you don't like the food
   d. other _____

4. Your natural hair color is brown, but you decided to dye it blond. Instead of blond, though, your hair turned bright orange. What would you do?
   a. try to color your hair again
   b. leave your hair orange
   c. shave your head
   d. other _____

5. You have an early breakfast meeting at work. You oversleep and get to work late. What would you say?
   a. your bus broke down
   b. you overslept
   c. you thought the meeting was tomorrow
   d. other _____

Activity 2: Who's telling the truth?

A Think of an emergency situation that has happened to you (an accident, childhood illness, a fire, a time you got lost, etc.). Write one sentence about what happened.

B Group work. Get into a group of three people and follow the directions below.

1. Compare the sentences you wrote in A. Choose *one* to talk about.
2. The person whose story it is will tell the other two group members about the event. They have three minutes to ask questions and learn as much about the event as possible.

C Group work. Get together with another group of three people. Follow the directions.

Group A: All three people say the sentence chosen in B. Each person should try to get Group B to think that the event happened to him or her.

Group B: Ask questions. Try to figure out who is telling the truth and who isn't. When you've finished asking questions, guess who is telling the truth. Explain your answer. Group A tells you if you're right or wrong.

I think Carlos is telling the truth because he said that he'd taken skating lessons as a child . . .

D Group work. Change roles and do exercise C again.

 **Check out the CNN® video.**   **Practice your English online at** <u>elt.heinle.com/worldpass</u>

Unit 12: Emergency!

A There are many hazards in nature. Match the words on the left with the correct description.
Circle the ones that have occurred in your country.

1. landslide ___
2. tsunami ___
3. earthquake ___
4. volcanic eruption ___
5. flash flood ___
6. tornado ___
7. blizzard ___
8. hurricane ___

a. a bad winter storm with heavy snow and strong winds
b. a storm with very strong winds that moves over the ocean
c. a sudden and rapid rising and overflowing of water onto dry land
d. a violent storm over land with air that spins and destroys things
e. a sudden shaking of the earth's surface
f. the sudden falling of mud, rocks, or dirt down a hill or mountain
g. a huge ocean wave caused by a volcanic eruption or an earthquake
h. gas, steam, and melted rock exploding from a mountain

B A first aid kit is a box that contains supplies to treat people who have a sudden injury or illness.
Read the contents of the kit and decide what you would use for each situation below.

> ### FIRST AID KIT CONTENTS
> | | | | |
> |---|---|---|---|
> | thermometer | elastic bandage | scissors | ointment |
> | pain reliever | tweezers | antiseptic | |

1. My little boy's face feels very hot. I wonder if he has a fever? _____
2. I have a terrible headache. _____
3. I was playing soccer and I sprained my ankle. It hurts when I walk. _____
4. There's a little piece of wood stuck in my finger. I need to pull it out. _____
5. An insect bit me and it itches a lot. _____
6. My daughter was playing and she fell on her knee. Now it's scraped and dirty. _____
7. I need to cut off a piece of this tape. _____

C Study the word combinations. Use the correct form of each phrase to complete the sentences.

> Word combinations with *danger*
>
> | | |
> |---|---|
> | in danger | a serious/real danger |
> | put someone in danger | There's no danger of that! |
> | to be in danger of (doing something) | be a danger to |
> | out of danger | |

1. That building was so badly damaged in the earthquake that it _____ collapsing.
2. Rescuers got the passengers off of the sinking ship and brought them to shore, so they are _____ now.
3. A truck broke down in the middle of the highway. It _____ other vehicles where it is now.
4. My lazy brother is never going to get a job. _____.
5. The growth of cities is _____ to many species of animals that live in the surrounding countryside.
6. The refugees say that their lives will be _____ in their home country.
7. By driving too fast with her children in the car, she _____ them _____.

I didn't know that!

The term *get fired* arose centuries ago when villagers wanted to drive an unwanted person out of the settlement but did not feel the person should be killed. They would set fire to the person's home in order to make them leave. Hence the phrase *get fired* became synonymous with being asked to leave.

D Many people organize items in their homes in preparation for an emergency.
Classify these items in the correct categories, using your dictionary as necessary.

cereal	insurance papers	flashlight	plastic sheeting
hammer and nails	passports	crackers	whistle
screwdriver	canned goods	fire extinguisher	birth certificates
bank account numbers	bottled water	heavy tape	first aid kit

Food and drink	Safety equipment	Tools and supplies	Important documents

In Other Words

Help is the most general term: *I'll help you cook dinner tonight.*
Assist is more formal or technical: *Volunteers assisted the police in searching for the lost child.*
Lend a hand is informal: *Hey, Pete, can you lend a hand with these heavy boxes?*
Help out is also informal: *I don't usually work at the store. I just help out when they're very busy.*

Frightened means feeling fear: *I felt frightened when I heard the wind getting stronger.*
Scared is informal and often used by children: *Daddy, I'm scared of that dog!*
If you are terrified, you feel extreme fear: *I was terrified when the plane began to fall.*

fearful and fearsome
If you are *fearful*, you are afraid of many things.
If you are *fearsome*, you make other people feel afraid!
The fearful little boy always cried when he was outdoors.
The fearsome little boy always cried when he was outdoors.

Expansion Pages

Review: Units 10–12

1 LANGUAGE CHECK

On a separate sheet of paper, rewrite the sentences using the words in parentheses and making all necessary changes.

1. The children don't have any money, so they can't go to the movie. (if they)
2. Is there a final exam in this class? (do you know)
3. "I need to get to the library before it closes." (he said that)
4. I don't have a big house, so I can't have any pets. (if I)
5. When does the flight to Sydney leave? (can you tell me)
6. Did I turn the stove off before I went out? (I wonder)
7. Are there any inexpensive hotels near the airport? (do you have any idea)
8. "If I don't have time to cook, I'll bring home a pizza." (she said that)
9. I didn't know you were coming to the party, so I didn't offer you a ride. (if I)
10. "The weather should be better by the weekend." (the forecaster said that)
11. He got in an accident because the road was slippery. (if the road)

2 VOCABULARY CHECK

Choose the correct answer.

1. It's a ____ hotel, and every room has its own private garden.
   a. primitive b. deluxe c. run-of-the-mill
2. After a hurricane warning, you should ____ the extent of damage immediately.
   a. consider b. give c. take
3. We really hit it ____ on our first date, and sat talking like old friends.
   a. off b. up c. on
4. My sister is planning to bum ____ Europe during her summer vacation.
   a. along b. above c. around
5. I'm not really a ____ traveler. This will be my first trip overseas.
   a. seasoned b. budget c. primitive
6. John and I are very ____. We're both very active and love to be outdoors.
   a. controlling b. compatible c. committed
7. Becky fell head over ____ in love with her boyfriend the first time she met him.
   a. heart b. feet c. heels
8. Alia ____ time off from work to visit her parents every summer.
   a. takes b. puts c. gives
9. During the flood, many families were forced to ____ their homes and move to a safer place.
   a. jeopardize b. evacuate c. ascertain
10. I wanted to buy a motorcycle, but that didn't go ____ too well with my parents.
    a. through b. over c. about
11. You need to have a back-____ light in case the electricity goes off.
    a. up b. down c. over
12. This is the most ____ island I've ever seen. There are no trees or plants—just bare rocks.
    a. thrilling b. desolate c. memorable
13. Luis is still angry at his old girlfriend because she cheated ____ him with a good friend.
    a. on b. from c. to
14. Many countries have emergency ____ systems for natural disasters.
    a. telling b. advising c. warning

3 NOW YOU'RE TALKING!

Situation 1

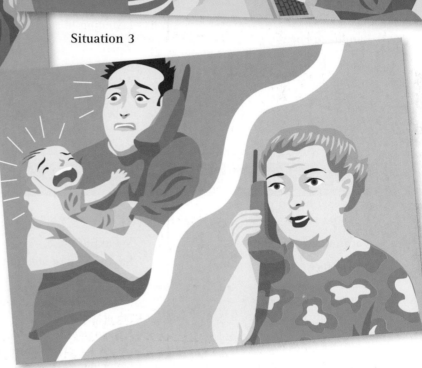

Situation 2

Situation 3

A Pair work. Choose one of the pictures and imagine yourselves in the situation. What would the people talk about? Briefly review the language notes from Units 10–12.

B Pair work. Read the statements in C and add two of your own goals. Then role-play the situation you chose keeping your speaking goals in mind.

C Now rate your speaking. Use + for good, ✓ for OK, and − for things you need to improve.

How did you do?	
I spoke loudly enough for my partner(s) to hear me.	
I spoke without too much hesitation.	
I spoke at a good rate of speed—not too fast or too slow.	
I used new vocabulary from the units.	
I used at least three expressions from the units.	
I practiced the grammar from the units.	
My own goals: 1. _____ 2. _____	

Language Summaries

Unit 1 *What's the Story?*

Lesson A

Vocabulary Focus

alter
cover
go after
go over
interpret
make up
piece together
verify

Additional Vocabulary

change a / one's story
kill a story

Language Focus

Review of the simple past and present perfect

Speaking:
Telling stories

I'll never forget the time . . .
Did I ever tell you about the time . . .
A couple of years ago . . .
Last summer . . .
It happened when . . .
One night . . .
All of a sudden . . .
Suddenly . . .
What happened in the end was . . .
In the end . . .
Looking back on it, . . .
It seems funny now, but . . .

Listening to stories

Wow!
Really!
Are you kidding?
Are you joking?
Unbelievable!

And then what
  happened?
What did you do next?
Do you mean?
Did you say?

Lesson B

Vocabulary

consequences
expectantly
family
fate
magic charm
solemnly
sorry
stormy night
visitor
wish
your loss

Unit 2 *Technology*

Lesson A

Vocabulary Focus

dependence
impersonal
information overload
interaction
liberating
multitask
promote
recipe for disaster
sedentary

Additional Vocabulary

cure for
dealings with
dependence on
get to the bottom of
  (something)

Language Focus

Review of the passive voice

Speaking:
Saying you're able/not able to do something

I might be able to . . .
I'm pretty good at . . .
I haven't got a clue about . . .
I know something about . . .
I'm no good at . . .
I don't have the faintest idea.

Lesson B

Vocabulary

anonymously
at stake
automatically
benefit
device
display
embed
privacy
track
unique

Unit 3 *Personality*

Lesson A

Vocabulary Focus

control freak	overachiever
early riser	pushover
go-getter	risk taker
hothead	self-starter

Additional Vocabulary

even though
free spirit
heartbreaker
homebody
night owl
team player

Language Focus

Adverb clauses of contrast, purpose, and time

Speaking:
Making general statements

Generally speaking . . .
In general . . .
For the most part . . .
Typically . . .
As a rule . . .
Normally . . .

Lesson B

Vocabulary

assertive
driven
easygoing
introspective
let someone go
nurturing
optimistic
peaceful
refined
systematic
unpredictable

Unit 4 *Make an Impact*

Lesson A

Vocabulary Focus

activists
apathetic
aware
carry on this tradition
circumstances
escapist
generation
issues
motivated
visionary

Additional Vocabulary

amoral
apolitical
asocial
atypical
internship
slacker

Language Focus

Modals and phrasal modals

Speaking:
Exchanging ideas in a non-confrontational way

Exactly!
Definitely!
I completely agree.
You may be right about . . .
You're absolutely right!
You may have something there.

I hate to disagree with you, but . . .
I see your point, but . . .
I know what you mean, but . . .
You may be right in part, but . . .

Yeah, but I don't think so.
I'm not so sure about that.
I'm not sure I agree with you.

That seems a bit extreme.
Oh, come on!
No way!

Lesson B

Vocabulary

business as usual
do your part
hack into
promote
public service announcements
raise awareness
solution
speak out against
think outside the box

Language Summaries

Unit 5 *Believe It or Not*

Lesson A

Vocabulary Focus

authority	outcome
devoted	seemingly
distress call	vanished
document	sought
evidence	strand
identify	theory
incident	witness
involvement	

Additional Vocabulary

adopt	premises
can't tell two	run into
people apart	to say the least
have a lot	twist of fate
in common	whereabouts
only child	
out of the ordinary	
outskirts	

Language Focus

Modals of speculation about the past

Speaking:
Making speculations

I wonder if . . .
I suppose . . .
I suspect that . . .
I'm pretty sure that . . .
I'm convinced/certain/positive that . . .
It's impossible that . . .
There's no doubt that . . .

Responding to speculations

Definitely!
You're probably right.
You may be right.
Well, maybe, but . . .
That hardly seems likely.
No way! (informal)

Lesson B

Vocabulary

inexplicable
intuition
malfunction
observe
previous
routinely
speculate
trigger

Unit 6 *Today's Workplace*

Lesson A

Vocabulary Focus

catch on	go under
come up with	hand in
cut back on	lay off
figure out	pass over
find out	set up
get ahead	stick with
give up	take off

Additional Vocabulary

get away
get back to
get by
get into
goof off
got behind

Language Focus

Phrasal verbs

Speaking:
Negotiating a solution

Would you consider . . . if I . . .
If you'll . . . I could . . .
Bear in mind . . .
Remember that . . .
I can agree to that.
That will be fine.
That's not possible.
I'm afraid I can't.

Lesson B

Vocabulary

an opportunity in disguise
come around
have butterflies in (one's) stomach
so to speak

Unit 7 *Does Crime Pay?*

Lesson A

Vocabulary Focus

behind bars	imprison
colleague	legitimate
fundamental	offense
get away with	outrageous
illegal	punish

Additional Vocabulary

a real gray area
a red alert
as white as a sheet
on the black market
the black sheep of the family
pickpocket
see red

Language Focus

The past perfect

Speaking:
Deciding what to do in a situation

We should probably . . .
Don't you think we ought to . . .
Let's just . . .
It seems to me . . .
Look at it this way . . .
If we . . . then . . .
If we were . . .

Lesson B

Vocabulary

abduct
accomplice
apprehend
capture
charge
conduct an investigation
disorderly conduct
hold up
kidnap
kidnappers
law enforcement officials
mastermind
prankster
rob
terrorize
troublemaker

Unit 8 *Big Spender*

Lesson A

Vocabulary Focus

benefit	pay off
get my finances in order	put away
get out of debt	reward
invest	run out
live paycheck to paycheck	splurge
	squander
make ends meet	stick to a budget
max out	sustain

Additional Vocabulary

over/underachiever
over/underbooked
over/undercharged
over/underestimated
over/underfeed(s)
over/underpaid
over/underpriced
over/underutilized

Language Focus

Gerunds and infinitives

Speaking:
Making suggestions

Why don't you . . .
How about . . .
Have you thought about . . .
Have you considered . . .
What if you . . .
Maybe you should . . .
You could . . .

Lesson B

Vocabulary

economy
emigrate
immigrant
migrate
mobile
opportunity
start from scratch
worth it

Language Summaries

Unit 9 *Family Matters*

Lesson A

Vocabulary Focus

bewilder
bicultural
bring up
clash
close-knit
conflict

extended family
isolate
look after
raise
take care of
upbringing

Additional Vocabulary

adoptive family
biological family
immediate family
nuclear family
snap decision
to talk it through

Language Focus

Subjective relative clauses

Speaking:
Stating and rebutting a case

The fact of the matter is . . .
It's clear that . . .
You can't deny that . . .
Well, I don't think . . .
It's obvious that . . .

Some people say . . . / But . . .
It may seem that . . . / But actually . . .
A lot of people think . . . / But in reality . . .
A lot of people think . . . / But on the other
  hand . . .

Lesson B

Vocabulary

conventional
in the same boat
killing
pool
stand by
turn to

Unit 10 *Travel & Vacation*

Lesson A

Vocabulary Focus

blow
book
breathtaking
desolate
memorable
money
overrun with
  tourists

primitive
remote
rough it
run-of-the-mill
seasoned traveler
wander off the
  beaten path

Additional Vocabulary

adventurous
charter
experienced
fend for oneself
guided
hindsight

in hindsight
nonstop
sightseeing
turbulent
whirlwind

Language Focus

Embedded questions

Speaking:
**Explaining plans and making travel
suggestions**

Here's the plan/idea.
One option is . . . Another option is . . .
What we have in mind is . . .
Considering that . . .
I'm considering . . .
Keep in mind that . . .

Lesson B

Vocabulary

bum around
constructively
putting off
take it easy
take time off

Unit 11 *Men & Women*

Lesson A

Vocabulary Focus

bachelor	hit it off
browsing	ideal
calling the shots	not go over
cheat on	reluctant
chemistry	uninhibited
compatible	
eligible	
fall head over heels	

Additional Vocabulary

firefighter
flight attendant
foot the bill (for something)
mail carrier
supervisor
turnoff

Language Focus

Present and past unreal conditionals

Speaking:

Making and responding to invitations

Let me think about it.
I'd love to.
Can I get back to you about that later?
How about another day?
I'm busy then.
I'll have to check my calendar.
Sure, sounds good.
I'm afraid I can't.

Lesson B

Vocabulary

blown away
commitment
dumped
etiquette
I'm into (something)
insensitive
It's up to you.
soulmate
pressuring

Unit 12 *Emergency!*

Lesson A

Vocabulary Focus

back-up plan	implement
devise	in-depth
essential	jeopardize
evacuation	on hand
evaluate	take into
extent	consideration
get through	walk through
hazard	warning systems

Additional Vocabulary

be cut out for	hazardous
(something)	jeopardize
evacuate	jeopardy
evacuation	poison
evaluate	poisonous
evaluation	summarize
hazard	summary

Language Focus

Reported speech

Speaking:

Dealing with a crisis situation

Don't worry.
Relax.
Nothing to worry about.
Hang in there.
Take it easy.
Don't get upset.
Everything's going to be OK.

What's the matter?
What does it look/sound like?
What happened after that?
Can you tell me exactly what happened?
What did you do then?
What happened?

The first/next thing to do is . . .
You'd better . . .
Why don't you try . . .
You need to . . .

How is he/she/it now?
What's happening now?
Did that work?
Is it any better?

Lesson B

Vocabulary

also
beat the odds
but unlike
devastated
emerged
fled
like
nevertheless
retreated
though
whereas
wiped out

Grammar Summaries

Unit 1 *What's the Story?*

Language Focus: Review of the simple past and present perfect

Use the simple past to talk about actions that began and ended in the past. Use the present perfect for actions that began in the past and continue in the present:

My father **was** a reporter for thirty years. (He's retired now.)
My mother **has been** a reporter for thirty years. For the past 10 years, **she's worked** for *The Daily Standard*.
(She is still working as a reporter.)

If a specific time is mentioned in the past, use the simple past. If the time when something happened isn't mentioned, use the present perfect:

Have you ever **been** to Asia?   Yes, I **visited** Japan and Korea last year.
                                        Yes, I**'ve visited** both Japan and Korea.

Use the present perfect for past actions that have a connection to a present result:

The test **hasn't started** yet. We're still waiting for the teacher to arrive.

The adverbs *already, just, never, still,* and *yet* are often used with the present perfect. Some adverbs can also be used with the simple past with no change in meaning:

I've *never* **been** there, but I'd like to visit.
Bill *still* **hasn't phoned**. I hope he's OK.
Have you finished your homework *yet?* = Did you finish your homework yet?
Let me introduce Mia.   That's OK, we**'ve** *already* **met**. = That's OK, we already **met**.
Their plane **has** *just* **landed**. = Their plane just **landed**.

Unit 2 *Technology*

Language Focus: Review of the passive voice

Tense	Active Voice	Passive Voice
present	People in Morocco *speak* Arabic and French.	Arabic and French **are spoken** in Morocco.
present continuous	They*'re building* a new library on campus.	A new library **is being built** on campus.
present perfect	The airlines *have canceled* all flights due to bad weather.	All flights **have been canceled** due to bad weather.
past	The police *arrested* twenty people at yesterday's demonstration.	Twenty people **were arrested** at yesterday's demonstration.
future with *will*	The embassy *will mail* your visa to you.	Your visa **will be mailed** to you.

In a passive sentence, the object of an active sentence becomes the subject:

          subject   object   subject   agent
ACTIVE: <u>Willem Kolff</u> **invented** <u>the first artificial heart</u>.   PASSIVE: <u>The first artificial heart</u> **was invented** by <u>Willem Kolff</u>.

The agent is not always used in passive sentences. It is omitted when the agent is unknown, obvious, or has been previously mentioned. Also, it can be omitted to avoid having to say it:

The mail **is delivered** at noon every day.
Professor Hu told us about the final exam. The format of the exam **was explained** in detail.
The store **was robbed** last night. We don't know who did it.

You can use the agent, especially if it gives additional or surprising information:

Several of today's household appliances **were invented** in the early twentieth century <u>by women</u>.

Unit 3 *Personality*

Language Focus: Adverb clauses of purpose, contrast, and time

Adverb clauses are dependent clauses. (They cannot stand alone and need a main clause to complete the sentence's meaning.) Adverb clauses answer the questions *why, when, how,* or *where* something happened:

      main clause   adverb clause
    I left the party early <u>because</u> I wasn't feeling well.

When the adverb clause comes before the main clause, put a comma after it:
    Because I wasn't feeling well, I left the party early.

Adverb clauses that show a reason or purpose for doing something (with *because, since,* and *so that*) answer the question *why*:
    I can't go out tonight **because / since** I have a lot of homework. (= reason for doing something)
    I took the early bus **so (that)** I could get to class on time. (= purpose for doing something)

In conversation, an adverb clause with *because* can stand alone to emphasize the reason for doing something. *Since* cannot be used in this way:
    Why are you leaving?   **Because I'm tired.** [~~Since I'm tired.~~]

Adverb clauses of time (with *when* or *whenever*) answer the question *when*. Often, *when* and *whenever* both mean "every time that something happens." Use *when* if the meaning is "at the specific time that something happened":
    When(ever) I have to speak in front of the class, I get nervous.
    When Jamie called yesterday morning, I was sleeping. (~~Whenever Jamie called~~ . . .)

Adverb clauses of opposition or contrast (with *though, although,* and *even though*) are used to introduce a different or surprising idea. The words can be used with no change in meaning:
    Although / Even though / Though the cell phone was expensive, I bought it anyway.

Despite the fact (that) can also be used to introduce an adverb clause of contrast:
    Despite the fact that he lied to me, I still consider Darin to be my best friend.

Unit 4 *Make an Impact*

Language Focus: Modals and phrasal modals

Can and *be able to* are used to talk about ability. When speaking about something that took place in the past, use *could* to say someone was able to do something in general at any time. Use *was/were able to* to indicate someone managed to do something:
    Can you ski?
    She **could** read music by the time she was three.
    He **was able to** finish the race in under an hour. (~~He could finish the race~~ . . .)

We can also talk about ability using *know how to*:
    Do you **know how to** speak Russian?

May and *can* are often used to give permission, but *can* is more informal:
    You **may** use your dictionaries to complete this exercise.
    You **can** stay as late as you'd like. Just don't forget to turn off the lights when you leave.

There is no past form of *may* for giving permission. Notice the past forms:
    You **may / You're allowed to** park here after 7 P.M.
    He said you **could / were allowed to** park here after 7 P.M.

Must expresses an obligation or sense of urgency. *Have to* is more commonly used to express necessity. (There is no past form of *must* for expressing necessity. Use *had to* instead.)

It's not safe here. Everyone **must** leave the building immediately.

At the lecture last night, I **had to** show my identification card to enter the building.

Should have is used to show regret about the past:

I'm too busy to take a vacation. I **should've** gone to Hawaii when I had the chance.

Be supposed to can be used to talk about what you should or shouldn't do:

What are you doing at home? **Aren't** you **supposed to** be at work today?

You**'re not supposed to** use your cell phone here.

Unit 5 *Believe It or Not*

Language Focus: Modals of speculation about the past

We use *could have, might (not) have,* and *may (not) have* to make a guess about a situation in the past, based on partial information:

The ancient tribes disappeared over 800 years ago. They **may have died** from starvation or
they **could have been killed** by disease. No one knows for sure.

Ben **might not have gone** to bed yet. It looks like his bedroom light is still on.

Use *must have* when you are sure of your guess:

The robbery **must have been** an inside job. There was no sign of forced entry.

Couldn't have and *can't have* indicate that the speaker thinks something is extremely unlikely or impossible:

Bill **couldn't have driven** his car to work today. It's being repaired.

Unit 6 *Today's Workplace*

Language Focus: Phrasal verbs

Phrasal verbs are two-word and three-word verbs. They are made up of a verb + a particle. Some common particles are: *about, ahead, down, in, on, off, over, out, under,* and *up.*

When combined with a verb, the particle can change the meaning of the verb phrase:

   give = to offer something   *give up* = to quit doing something

Two-word transitive verbs (taking a direct object)		Two-word intransitive verbs (not taking a direct object)		Three-word verbs
carry out	put off	catch on	give up	come up with
cut back (on)	set up	get ahead	go under	get back to (someone)
figure out	stick with	get away	goof off	
hand in	think about	get behind	hang on	
lay off		get by	take off (*increase*)	
		get in		

Unit 7 *Does Crime Pay?*

Language Focus: The past perfect

The simple past is used to describe an event in the past. When there are two events in the past, the past perfect is used to describe the event that happened earlier:

They <u>showed</u> me her photo. Suddenly, I realized I **had met** her before.
Before Mario and Carla <u>visited</u> Korea, they**'d** never **eaten** kimchi.
I **hadn't finished** cleaning when the first guest <u>arrived</u>.

Before, after, when, until, already, and *by the time* are often used with the past perfect:

I**'d** *already* **found** a job three months *before* I graduated from college.
Chris **hadn't seen** snow *until* he moved to Boston.
By the time we reached the summit, the weather **had changed**.

The past perfect may be optional when the sequence of events is clear from the sentence. In these cases, use the simple past for both actions. (This is often true with the words *before* and *after*.)

After our team <u>scored</u> the winning goal, the crowd <u>went</u> wild.

Unit 8 *Big Spender*

Language Focus: Gerunds and infinitives

A **gerund** is the *–ing* form of a verb (e.g., *saving*). It functions like a noun and can be the subject, the direct object, or the object of a preposition. An **infinitive** is *to* + the base form of a verb (e.g., *to borrow*). It is often used as a direct object.

Some verbs and verb phrases are followed only by a gerund. Some can only take the infinitive:

Verbs followed by gerund only I *don't mind* **loaning** you some money.	Verbs followed by infinitive only I *managed* **to save** some money last month.
discuss, dislike, don't mind, enjoy, feel like, go, mind, quit, recall, recommend, suggest, understand	*agree, appear, demand, fail, intend, manage, offer, plan, promise, seem, wait*

Verb + preposition + gerund I *plan on* **donating** some money to charity.	Be + adjective + preposition + gerund I*'m good at* **budgeting** money.
agree on, ask about, believe in, care about, depend on, feel about, insist on, object to, plan on, talk about	*be afraid of, be careful about, be good at, be guilty of, be happy about, be interested in, be used to, be worried about*

Verbs such as *attempt, begin, can't stand, continue, hate, like, love, prefer, propose, regret, start,* and *try* can be followed by either a gerund or an infinitive with no change in meaning:

I'm impatient. I *hate* **waiting** in line. (= I *hate* **to wait** in line.)

Verbs such as *stop, remember,* and *forget* can take either the gerund or infinitive, but the meaning changes depending on which is used:

I stopped **to drink** a soda. (I paused what I was doing so I could drink a soda.)
I stopped **drinking** soda. (I used to drink soda, but I don't anymore.)

Unit 9 *Family Matters*

Language Focus: Subject relative clauses

Who, that, and *which* are called subject relative pronouns. They are used to introduce relative clauses. The relative clause defines or gives more information about the noun that it follows. It is a dependent clause—it cannot stand alone:

Here are the photos **that I took last summer.**
Her dog, **which is a very expensive breed,** is not very friendly.

The verb following the subject relative pronoun agrees with the noun it is modifying:

I know the <u>woman</u> who <u>lives</u> next door.   I know the <u>women</u> who <u>live</u> next door.

There are two different kinds of relative clauses with subject relative pronouns: defining and non-defining. A defining relative clause cannot be omitted because it is needed to make the meaning of the sentence clear. Defining relative clauses are often used to give definitions:

The bus **that goes downtown** is the number 48.
A geologist is a scientist **who studies rocks and soil.**

A non-defining relative clause can be omitted because it only adds extra information. The meaning of the sentence is clear even without it. Notice the use of commas in writing (which are marked by pauses in speech):

Jason, **who got married last year,** was my best friend all through high school.

A relative clause can also show possession with *whose*:

I have a friend. Her brother is a famous artist.
I have a friend **whose brother is a famous artist.**

Unit 10 *Travel & Vacation*

Language Focus: Embedded questions

An embedded question is a question that is part of another sentence. It can appear inside a statement or a question. Notice the word order and punctuation in these embedded questions:

Direct question	Embedded questions
Where is the bank?	Can you tell me **where the bank is?**
	I wonder **where the bank is.**

Embedded *yes/no* questions begin with *if* or *whether*:

Direct question	Embedded questions
Does the bus stop here?	I'd like to know **if the bus stops here.**
	Do you know **whether (or not) the bus stops here?**

Embedded questions are often used to ask for information politely and to say we don't know the answer to something:

Excuse me. Do you happen to know **what time it is?**
I don't know **why the flight was canceled.**

Embedded questions follow expressions like these:

Can/Could you tell me . . . ?	*I don't know . . .*
Do you have any idea . . . ?	*I wonder/was wondering . . .*
Do you know . . . ?	*I'd like to know . . .*
I can't say . . .	*I'm not sure . . .*
I don't have any idea . . .	*It's not clear . . .*

Unit 11 *Men & Women*

Language Focus: Present and past unreal conditionals

We use unreal conditionals to talk about situations that are improbable, imaginary, or past events that never occurred.

    if **clause**   **result clause**
    If I lived in Hawaii, I'd go surfing every day. (But I don't live in Hawaii now . . .)
    If I had lived in Hawaii, I would have gone surfing every day. (But I didn't live in Hawaii in the past . . .)

Use the present unreal conditional for present and future situations. In the *if* clause, the verb is in the simple past. Use *would* + verb in the result clause. (Use *could* to show that something is possible.) Notice the comma when the *if* clause comes before the result clause:

    If I <u>lived</u> in the country, <u>I'd have</u> less stress in my life. (I'd = I would)
    I would stay and talk if I <u>didn't have</u> class now.
    I <u>could sleep</u> later every morning if I <u>lived</u> closer to the office.

If I were you, . . . is used to give advice. (When *be* appears in the *if* clause, use *were* for all subjects.)
    If I were you, I'd call the police.

Use the past unreal conditional for situations that never happened. In the *if* clause, the verb is in the past perfect. Use *would have* + verb in the result clause. If you're uncertain about the result, use *might have* or *could have*:

    If <u>I'd won</u> the election last month, I <u>would've had</u> a big party to celebrate. (I'd = I had)
    They <u>might have survived</u> if they <u>'d run</u> faster.

Unit 12 *Emergency!*

Language Focus: Reported speech

Reported speech (also called *indirect speech*) is used to report what someone else has said:

    Quoted speech   **Reported speech**
    "I like jazz," he said.   He said (that) he **liked** jazz.

Reported speech uses a reporting verb (e.g., *say, admit, complain, explain, remark, report*). The verb following the reporting verb often shifts to a past form. Do not use quotation marks with reported speech:

    Quoted speech: "There **was** a lot of damage from the earthquake," she said.
    Reported speech: She said (that) there **had been** a lot of damage from the earthquake.

Pronouns and time adverbs also shift in reported speech:
    "<u>We</u> **will** win the championship <u>tomorrow</u>."
    <u>They</u> said (that) they **would** win the championship <u>the following day</u>.

Tense shift does not occur with certain modals (*could, should,* or *might*) or verb tenses:
    "You **shouldn't** get married," her parents said.   They said (that) she **shouldn't** get married.
    "I **had** already **gotten** married," she said.   She said (that) she **had** already **gotten** married.

You can also use reported speech for questions. Notice the statement word order in the reported question:
    Yes/No **question:** "Is it true?"   He asked if <u>it was true</u>.
    Wh- **question:** "What **are** they doing?"   She asked what <u>they were doing</u>.

Skills Index

Expansion Pages Answer Key

Unit 1
A. 1. d 2. e 3. c 4. a 5. b B. 1. end of story 2. It's the same old story. 3. to make a long story short 4. What's the story?
5. is a different story C. 1. anecdotes 2. tales 3. statement 4. yarns 5. a report 6. gossip 7. the fable 8. chronicle D. 1. fate
2. expectantly 3. firm 4. solemnly 5. consequences 6. spell

Unit 2
A. a trend toward, the current trend, the upward trend, buck the trend B. 1. a trend toward 2. reverse the trend 3. downward trend
4. economic trends 5. setting the trend C. 1. f 2. a 3. c 4. g 5. d 6. e 7. b D. 1. f 2. c 3. d 4. a 5. e 6. b E. 1. overdo it
2. overdue 3. overeat 4. overpowering 5. overlooked 6. overloaded

Unit 3
A. 1. a split personality 2. a personality clash 3. a sports personality 4. a strong personality 5. A personality disorder 6. personality
traits B. 1. j 2. e 3. d 4. g 5. a 6. f 7. i 8. h 9. b 10. c C. 1. overachiever 2. pushover 3. hothead 4. control freak
D. 1. driven 2. conflict 3. extrovert 4. loud 5. aloof 6. gloomy 7. cautious 8. disappointment E. 1. shouldn't 2. seldom 3. a lot
4. wasn't 5. together 6. pay more attention

Unit 4
A. 1. f 2. b 3. a 4. c 5. d 6. e B. 1. active 2. an activity 3. proactive 4. an activist 5. acting 6. activism C. 1. freezing 2. tiny
3. boiling 4. terrifying 5. enormous 6. horrendous 7. gorgeous D. 1. take action 2. swing into action 3. no further action is needed
4. put your ideas into action 5. call for action 6. plan of action E. 1. c 2. a 3. b 4. a 5. c

Unit 5
A. 1. e 2. f 3. d 4. a 5. c 6. b B. 1. clue, evidence 2. sleuth, investigator 3. puzzle, enigma 4. speculation, hypothesis C. 1. d
2. b 3. a 4. e 5. c D. 1. malcontent 2. malpractice 3. malfunction 4. malnourished 5. malformed 6. maltreat

Unit 6
A. 1. together 2. behind 3. around 4. into 5. around to 6. along with 7. off B. 1. bills 2. intern 3. take off 4. application 5. go
under 6. give up 7. customer 8. give up C. 1. d 2. e 3. a 4. b 5. f 6. c D. 1. Get to work! 2. We can work it out. 3. Everything
will work out. 4. Don't get all worked up about it. 5. you have your work cut out for you 6. it's in the works E. 1. e 2. h 3. g 4. d
5. b 6. a 7. f 8. c

Unit 7
A. 1. c 2. g 3. f 4. d 5. b 6. h 7. e 8. a B. 1. vandalism 2. speeding 3. shoplifting 4. arson 5. mugging 6. murder
7. robbery 8. burglary C. 1. b 2. e 3. a 4. d 5. c 6. f D. 1. against the 2. by 3. enforce the 4. became 5. obey the 6. breaks
the

Unit 8
A. 1. rent, mortgage payments 2. electricity, water 3. groceries, lunches at work 4. clothing, shoes 5. bus tickets, gasoline 6. student
loans, tuition 7. movies, hobbies B. 1. shopaholic, big spender, spendthrift 2. miser, tightwad, cheapskate, penny-pincher C. 1. E 2. I
3. I 4. E 5. E 6. E 7. I 8. I 9. E D. 1. at no extra cost 2. pay the cost 3. low-cost 4. rising cost 5. cost of living 6. the cost of

Unit 9
A. [row 1] adopt; adoption; [row 2] extended; extensive; [row 3] isolate; isolation 1. extended 2. Adoptive 3. isolation 4. isolated
5. adopted B. 1. e 2. d 3. c 4. b 5. a 6. f 7. g C. 1. reunion 2. man 3. names 4. tree 5. circle 6. room 7. doctor
D. 1. pooled 2. long-term 3. flat 4. rush 5. struggling 6. network 7. mobile 8. eventually E. 1. c 2. g 3. h 4. e 5. f 6. a 7. b
8. j 9. d 10. i

Unit 10
A. 1. a travel agency 2. traveler's checks 3. travel expenses 4. widely traveled 5. a travelogue 6. travel guide 7. traveling salesperson
B. 1. relaxing 2. intrigued 3. exhausting 4. thrilled C. 1. trekking 2. established 3. specific 4. passion 5. harvest 6. pursuit
7. Sustainable D. 1. on vacation 2. paid vacation 3. vacation spot 4. three-day vacation 5. a family vacation 6. take a vacation
7. winter vacation 8. a vacation home

Unit 11
A. 1. have 2. have 3. take 4. play 5. take 6. play 7. go 8. go 9. see 10. see 11. go B. 1. ex 2. acceptable 3. insensitive
4. impersonal 5. defended 6. silent 7. emotional C. 1. d 2. f 3. e 4. b 5. g 6. c 7. a D. 1. much loved 2. a love-hate
relationship 3. a love affair 4. love song 5. a love triangle 6. a love story 7. is madly in love with 8. love child

Unit 12
A. 1. f 2. g 3. e 4. h 5. c 6. d 7. a 8. b B. 1. thermometer 2. pain reliever 3. elastic bandage 4. tweezers 5. ointment
6. antiseptic 7. scissors C. 1. was in danger of 2. out of danger 3. is a danger to 4. There's no danger of that! 5. a serious/real danger
6. in danger 7. puts, in danger D. Food and drink: cereal, canned goods, bottled water, crackers; Safety equipment: fire extinguisher,
first aid kit; Tools and supplies: hammer and nails, screwdriver, flashlight, heavy tape, plastic sheeting, whistle; Important documents:
bank account numbers, insurance papers, passports, birth certificates